William James
and
Phenomenology

Studies in Phenomenology and Existential Philosophy

William James
and
Phenomenology

James M. Edie

INDIANA UNIVERSITY PRESS

BLOOMINGTON AND INDIANAPOLIS

For my parents

Manufactured in the United States of America

Library of Congress Cataloging-in-Publication Data

Edie, James M.
William James and phenomenology.

(Studies in phenomenology and existential philosophy)
Bibliography: p.
Includes index.
1. James, William, 1842–1910. 2. Phenomenology.
I. Title. II. Series.
B945.J24E35 1987 191 86-45894
ISBN 0-253-36570-8
ISBN 0-253-20419-4 (pbk.)

1 2 3 4 5 91 90 89 88 87

Contents

Introduction

One of the purposes of these studies is to bring to the fore the importance of the philosophical thought of William James for the development of Edmund Husserl's phenomenology. As I stress in Chapter II, there can now be no doubt whatever that Husserl developed a number of his ideas on the intentionality of consciousness and on the ideal objectivity of the "objects of thought" by reading James, particularly the James of the *Principles*. I myself first came to James *from* Husserl (and Schutz and Gurwitsch, two of Husserl's disciples and commentators whom he himself trusted above all the others). For many years now we have been told by Dagfinn Føllesdal, Hubert Dreyfus, and some of their students that it was Gottlob Frege whose influence on Husserl was profound, even "traumatic," and that it was because of his criticism of *Philosophie der Arithmetik* that Husserl came to understand the sense-reference distinction properly. But this distinction can be found in Husserl prior to his reading of or contact with Frege. Now that J. N. Mohanty has proven beyond a shadow of a doubt[1] that Husserl developed his own theory of the intended object independently of Frege, we are free to give James his rightful place at the origins of the theory of intentionality. Of course, we should not exaggerate this influence, but it was certainly there, certainly as important for Husserl as Frege's, perhaps more important.

In my own career of teaching and reflection I have read the entire corpus of William James, but I must say that only the *Principles* and the *Varieties of Religious Experience* truly hold my attention, the first mainly for its theory of knowledge and the second because it is the first and really the only phenomenology of religious experience to have been written up to now, a subject in which Husserl himself was uninterested. This presents us with as magnificent an application of the phenomenological method to concrete detail as it is possible to find, including even those found later in Merleau-Ponty's various phenomenologies. James had a sense of phenomenological method long before the letter, and I hold his work up as a model.

There are, in fact, two major essays into phenomenology in James. The first, at the beginning of his career, is in "The Sentiment of Rationality." Here he gives us a veritable phenomenology not of reason, indeed, but of rationality. I deal with this in Chapter IV below. And, of course, the other great attempt at what I would call a true phenomenology (without, of course, the name—of which James knew nothing and which he would not have employed given his anti-Hegelian feelings) was in the *Varieties of Religious Experience,* which I deal with in Chapter III below.

At the present time there is a renewal of interest in the thought of William James which comes much less from the native traditions of the development of American philosophy than from phenomenology, on the one hand, and "critical theory," on the other. For this latter we have, as a publicist, mainly Richard Rorty to thank. Unlike the phenomenological revival of interest in James, the interest of the critical theorists and deconstructionists is centered on James's pragmatic theory of truth, especially as it was later interpreted by John Dewey.

As the reader of this volume will see, I largely pass over, though I do not totally dismiss, James's pragmatic theory of truth. It can, no doubt, be given an acceptable philosophical formulation[2] but it must be admitted that James himself, particularly in his popular pragmatist essays, nowhere gives us such an exposition, at least not in a systematic manner. In his prolific "middle" period (between the *Principles* and the *Varieties*) he writes as a relativist, for the most part consigning truth to some historical process which we can sense perhaps but for which we will never have any guarantee "until all of experience shall have taken place." He *does* sound like Heidegger and Dewey in many passages and that is why Rorty mentions him at all and why he is, almost unintentionally, now responsible for a new interest in James's thought. Merleau-Ponty, the phenomenologist, would say of the pragmatic theory of truth what James himself would have said at the time of the *Principles:* that it confuses the apodictic truth of reason with the more or less adequate truth of perception and the realms of experience about which we can have not absolute but only "presumptive" certainty.[3]

Rorty's holy trinity in his most imposing book, *Philosophy and the Mirror of Nature,*[4] consists of Dewey, Heidegger, and Wittgenstein. They and some of their followers get three-fourths of the book; other philosophers, about twenty-five pages.[5] In this connection it is interesting to remark that both Heidegger and James, when they occur, are interpreted at Rorty's hands in a Deweyan manner. An independent James does not speak for himself from Rorty's pages. There is an even more curious aspect of Rorty's deconstructionist prose (I will not even mention the continual grouping of Husserl and Russell together): he never mentions James without joining him to Nietzsche as if there were the closest and most profound unity of mind and thought between them. One should not completely forget that James himself, in one of his own rare references to Nietzsche, said that Nietzsche's thought reminded him of nothing so much as "the sick shriekings of a dying rat."[6]

The fact of the matter is that James's pragmatism is not that of John Dewey's experimentalism or of Heidegger's *Lichtungen;* James frequently, but especially in Chapter XXVIII of the *Principles*, gives purely linguistic and conceptual arguments the way Aristotle and Husserl did, based on "our insight into the very meaning of the word is,"[7] etc. I deal with this particularly in Chapters I and II but occasionally throughout the essays in this book. Though James at first *tried* to eschew metaphysics and epistemology (words he uses almost interchangeably when he gets around to them), ultimately he always comes back to them in the sense of coming back to the foundations. In 1888, when he was finishing the *Principles*, he wrote to the positivist psychologist Ribot:

> Empirical facts without "metaphysics" will always make a confusion and a muddle. I'm sorry to hear you still disparage metaphysics so much, since rightly understood, the word means only the search for *clearness* where common people do not even suspect that there is any lack of it. The ordinary positivist has simply a bad and muddled metaphysics which he refuses to criticize or discuss.[8]

James, like Husserl, was pretty much self-taught in the history of philosophy; the only degree James ever earned was in medicine and Husserl began as a mathematician who was dissatisfied with the practice of a mathematics which remained unaware of its transcendental foundations. But both James and Husserl recognized in some way— Husserl no doubt better than James with his Yankee hostility to German idealism—that all the recognized giants (Plato, Aristotle, Augustine, Aquinas, Descartes, Leibniz, Kant) of Western philosophy were "foundationalists" and their project could be called one of "foundationalism," if by that one means going to the very roots, logical origins, foundations of meaning and being. For all his later popular pragmatist essays, James never made reason dependent on something other than itself and would never have handed philosophy over to sociologists of knowledge and communications theorists. Though he did not like the term "transcendental," and most certainly not the word "phenomenology," I have tried to show in this book that it was integral to his own philosophy to go to the very roots of experience and knowledge, i.e., the ultimate logical conditions of their possibility. And that is what is meant by "transcendental."

In the *Principles* (see Chapter II) James attempted to follow out a thoroughgoing dualism and scientific realism only to find that he could not, for the simple reason that any scientific investigation makes philosophical presuppositions and, until these are clarified, the investigation is unfounded and blind. This is not to give some social preeminence to philosophers over social scientists or other scientists but to point out that they do different things.

Every factual science we know of originated from philosophy and was once a part of philosophy. The ancients knew this well; in thirteenth-century Paris one of the propositions students had to defend at their magisterial defense was that there is no science which is not a part of philosophy. This is evident in a historical sense even of the sciences which have most recently broken loose from philosophy, namely, psychology and linguistics. But physics, for instance, in the days of Newton, was not only a part of philosophy; it was also a part of natural theology. The history of the various sciences has shown that as soon as they have progressed to a stage of maturity, sufficiently advanced to develop their own distinctive methodologies they will be prosecuted by persons who no longer study philosophy *ex professo*. But they still make philosophical presuppositions. Aristotle discusses this frequently, mainly with examples from geometry; Aquinas makes it the cornerstone of the *Summa Theologiae*, where it takes up the *first* question of part one, even *before* he gets to the question of God.[9]

James also knew this or, rather, found it out—culminating in his famous Chapter XVIII of the *Principles* (which we discuss in Chapter I below). In short, no scientist or thinker can elaborate his thought in a systematic manner if he is to violate one single one of the laws of formal logic. Since the Greeks first discovered formal logic (what James calls "necessary truths"), it has been an integral part of philosophy and has been found to rule the textual discourse of all the disciplines. Only philosophers study logic *ex professo*, just as philosophers are the only ones to study structures of experience so fundamental that all persons and all sciences always already take them for granted. In this sense, as Husserl says in the *Fourth Investigation*, philosophy is rightly called the "science of trivialities."

Philosophy, therefore, does something different from any of the empirical sciences because it concentrates on the apriori, and on the conceptual. It can know that although no physicist or any other scientist studies the laws of logic, or the transcendental conditions of experience, as a part of his discipline (as Galen and Avicenna and Newton, for instance, still did), if in the course of elaborating his systematic and theoretical positions he should violate these laws, a scientist's theory will be subject to incoherence, contradiction, and error.

Where the James of history, and the James present in the following essays, differ from Rorty's Deweyan, Heideggerian, and Wittgensteinian pragmatism, deconstructionism, and relativism is, for one thing, in refusing to agree to allow philosophy to be parcelled out among a number of ill-defined empirical disciplines, thereby losing sight of the apriori and necessary truths which are the only thing truly "philosophical" about philosophy. As a physiologist, then a psychologist, then a philosopher, James knew as well as the phenomenologists that the mind of man has long been interested, for instance, in the brain, in how it works and how it can be studied. Several empirical sciences have been invented to study the brain. On the other hand, the brain, for its part, has not the slightest interest in or ability to study the mind. Philosophy, as our common ancestor, Socrates, taught us is a study of the mind (*nous*).

For Rorty, though not for James, bedrock is "the conversation of mankind" (for which he sometimes substitutes "the conversation of the West"). The main trouble with this is that a conversation is always a discourse, a spoken or written text, and a text makes certain formal presuppositions. It must be composed of a string of meaningful sentences, laid out in time if spoken, put down from left to right (or in some notational system) if written. There are dependent or incomplete meanings such as words, and then there are words grammatically formed in complete and independent units of meaning which we call sentences. But it is not enough for these sentences to be meaningful in themselves; they cannot follow one another in random order. They have to be organized into paragraphs, ultimately texts; they must, minimally, be compatible with one another, go together, pertain to the same domain of discourse, and, usually, more stringently, must imply one another, must follow from one another, must, in a word, make sense, perhaps even an argument. Finally, they may be testable as to their truth or falsity, whether it is merely to "ring true," to teach us something about ourselves, interpersonal relations, or to relate the kind of scientific observation which, as James has it, "plays into logic's hands." The point is that all these presuppositions are conceptual presuppositions and matters of logical form without which the unwitting "conversation of mankind" would be mere babble.

In short, as interesting as the deconstructionist effort is and as accidentally helpful as it may be for James studies, James is not on their side when it comes to making foundational truth a matter of social change, historical circumstance, or the genetic endowment of the race. He writes, in the concluding part of Chapter XXVIII of the *Principles* to which we have frequently alluded here and will discuss in Chapter I below, after an exhaustive discussion: "so far as the *theoretic* part of our . . . mental structure goes. . . . It can be due neither to our own nor to our ancestors' experience."[10]

The chapters of this book are essentially a reworking of previously published papers on the thought of William James as it relates to phenomenology. I have brought them together at the urging of friends, students, and colleagues to save them from being forever lost in out-of-date collections and journals, and I am happy to present them in this much more readily available form to persons interested in the subject at the present time.

Chapter I is taken from "Necessary Truth and Perception: William James and the Structure of Appearance," which first appeared in *New Essays in Phenomenology* (Chicago: Quadrangle Books, 1969), pp. 233–55.

Chapter II, "William James and Phenomenology," originally appeared in *The Review of Metaphysics*, March 1970, pp. 481–526.

Chapter III, "William James's Phenomenology of Religious Experience," was originally published in *American Philosophy and the Future*, edited by Michael Novak (New York: Charles Scribner's Sons, 1968), pp. 247–69.

Chapter IV is based on an article entitled "Notes on the Philosophical Anthropology of William James," which appeared in *An Invitation to Phenomenology* (Chicago: Quadrangle Books, 1965), pp. 110–32.

I would like herewith to thank the staff of the Indiana University Press for their great interest in my work, and for all the help and encouragement they have given over the years in publishing the series of Studies in Phenomenology and Existential Philosophy. I would also like to take this occasion to thank the secretaries of our department who have carried the brunt of the weight of typing all this material and getting it in proper shape for publication, namely, Audrey G. Thiel and Marina Pianu Rosiene.

William James
and
Phenomenology

I Necessary Truth and Perception: William James on the Structure of Experience

Recent research has begun to uncover a large number of themes in contemporary phenomenological thought which find parallels in the thought of William James.[1] Some of these can be traced to the direct influence of James on Husserl, but for the most part they transcend such direct historical interaction and rather show a common spirit and temper, developing independently but convergently toward the same goal—namely, the establishment of the bases for a method of *radical empiricism* in philosophy. This unattained goal, a radical philosophy of experience, has been the dream of many philosophers and philosophical schools, but it has remained up to the present time a largely unfulfilled hope. Empirio-criticists, positivists, pragmatists, and phenomenologists have all announced the program, but few have been able to flatter themselves at having accomplished more than a "beginning." One of the major philosophical problems which has always halted the initial empiricist thrust is the problem of accounting for our experience of "the kingdom of truth," as Husserl expressed it.

The question of the origin of categorial truth in experience is unsolved. Forbidden by the exigencies of its method from introducing any "metaphysical entities" into its explanations which cannot be justified within the texture of experience itself, phenomenology in particular is confronted with this problem. It preoccupied Husserl

1

throughout his life from the *Prolegomena* to *Erfahrung und Urteil;* Merleau-Ponty, who announced his program in the *Primacy of Perception* to examine "the relation between intellectual consciousness and perceptual consciousness" and to show how "ideal truth" is related to "perceived truth,"[2] died without writing the work which was to be entitled *L'Origine de la vérité.*[3]

Given the methodological similarities which have already been established between James on the one hand and such phenomenologists as Husserl and Merleau-Ponty on the other,[4] I believe it would be interesting and fruitful to examine how James approaches this particular question. I will, for the purposes of this discussion, postpone any elaborate treatment of his later "pragmatic theory of truth," which has so preoccupied his commentators, and instead go to the original sources of his later theories as they are given in the *Principles of Psychology,* his most important systematic treatise. We will find a striking similarity in the early Jamesian and the later phenomenological approach.

THE ORDERS OF REALITY AND THE PRIMACY OF THE PERCEPTUAL WORLD

It is a commonplace of phenomenology that any given act of consciousness is a highly complex and highly structured *synthesis* of elements and "forms" which, though they can be isolated for purposes of analysis, are given together inseparably in the unified whole which is an actual act of consciousness. Elements of "the imaginary," of "the fictive," of "the past," of the "historical," of the "cultural," of "the ideal," surround and are inextricably *given with* any complete act of perception, not to mention the qualities of feeling, mood, volition, or emotion such an act may contain as well. One of the chief tasks of phenomenology is precisely to *analyze* the complex intentional acts which are our experience of reality, to distinguish qualities, characters, and levels of such experience as they are inextricably given together. To say that such qualities, characters, and levels of consciousness have their own specificity, that they can be isolated from one another by analysis, that they can be distinguished within the pulsating flux of our conscious life is not to deny that, in actual experience, they are all inextricably given together and mutually implicate each other in our objectification of the world. The world as given to human consciousness, the world of "objects," is the world we experience *because* it is

different levels of discourse

the correlate of a consciousness which can simultaneously and succes-
sively live in "different orders of reality," in the perceptual, the imaginary, the ideal, etc. On the level of the prereflexive constitution of
reality, of our experience of the real world, our perceptual consciousness is a consciousness which anticipates (in operating imaginative
and fictive intentions) and retains (in operating memory intentions) its
world, which structures it in accord with past and anticipated experience, which "understands" it and "values" it by finding in it and *con-
ferring* on it a coefficient of ideality.

From the *Prolegomena* onward one of Husserl's constant doctrines
is that meaning and value are strictly correlative to factual experience,
that the meaning (or "essence") of an experience is that in terms of
which a given experience is structured by and for consciousness, that
meaning and fact are never separate in experience, since any essential
structure (i.e., that which is understood when one understands something in the flux of experience) is the meaning of the factual situation
of which it is the essence. The realm of prereflexive, prejudgmental
perceptual experience is "alive" with the "ideal" and with meaning.
The emergence of sense and meaning is not, thus, something reserved for the higher, fully reflexive acts of judging consciousness but
is immediately experienced prior to any theoretical reflection about
it. Meaning, he says, is "immanent" to experience on all its various levels, and there is a thread of intentional unity which binds the meanings given in perception to their correlates in imagination, memory,
and even in categorial thought.

Moreover, the most fundamental realm of meaning in which we
live is precisely the level of perceptual experience, of prethematic, operating intentions which form the foundation for later categorial acts
of reflection and imaginary reconstruction, etc. (the "active syntheses" of consciousness as opposed to the "passive" or "automatic syntheses" of prethematic perceptual awareness).

"It is *we* who are the genuine positivists,"[5] claims Husserl, and
Merleau-Ponty calls this thesis of the "primacy of perception" in the
orders of experience a "phenomenological positivism."[6] A large number of thinkers, beginning with William James, have asserted this thesis and attempted to outline its import and its consequences. James
speaks of the "paramount reality"[7] of the world of sensations and of the
"many worlds" or "sub-universes" built upon and surrounding it.
Straus speaks of "the primary world of the senses" as the source of all
"sense."[8] Schutz speaks of the "finite provinces of meaning" of "multi-

ple realities" centered around the "world of practical life" with its dominant "pragmatic motive,"[9] whereas Gurwitsch prefers the expression "orders of existence," which he conceives as meaning-contextures which analogously implicate each other on the fundamental basis of the contextures of perceptual experience.[10]

These differing terminologies ought not to confuse us, since all these thinkers recognize the intentional structure of experience and that the order of reality or existence with which we are dealing in perception, or in imagination, or in categorial thinking is strictly correlative to conscious acts. Thus whether we begin primarily with an intentional analysis of acts of consciousness (such as perceiving or imagining or thinking) or whether we turn our attention to the noematic correlates of such acts (the orders of reality or existence experienced as such), the one approach necessarily and correlatively implicates the other.

We can begin with James. Like Husserl, he distinguishes the world of "real existence" or "practical reality" from the other orders of "reality" whose distinctions are determined by the degree and kind of ego-involvement they express.

> *The fons et origo of all reality . . . is ourselves*. . . . The world of living realities as contrasted with unrealities is thus anchored in the Ego, considered as an active and emotional term. That is the hook from which the rest dangles, the absolute support. And as from a painted hook . . . one can only hang a painted chain, so conversely, from a real hook only a real chain can properly be hung. *Whatever things have intimate and continuous connection with my life are things of whose reality I cannot doubt*.[11]

The "paramount reality" is given to us through our perceptual insertion among other beings and objects in whom we have a practical and emotional involvement through our "tangible" relationships with them. It can be defined as the world within the reach of our senses, the world we can grasp immediately, upon which we can act and which can act upon us. Only a real dagger hurts when it is thrust into our flesh; only real poison can be taken into our mouths.[12] Within this world we are always situated in a *place* which is located by our bodily presence and from which all other objects and situations recede as from the zero point of a system of coordinates; our apprehension of the objects of our perceptual world is always perspectival, subject to further clarification and exploration. All together they constitute the indefinite horizon within which any present object emerges from a background of mutually implicating horizons which, at the limit, involve all other contemporaneously coexisting bodies in time and space. This world has a special temporal and spatial structure which is rooted in our own experience of temporality and spatiality. The experience of phenomenal time and phenomenal space gives us the primary conscious synthesis on the basis of which we can then construct the idea of "standard time," and the notion of "objective space." This is the world which we can never wholly escape; at every moment of our conscious lives we are subject to the laws of phenomenal time (the irreversible and temporally synthetic stream of consciousness), to the embodiment of consciousness in a perceptual space perspectivally related to other real beings.[13] While the perceptual world can never be experienced as a whole, and thus can never be given *as such*, it is nevertheless always *given with* any perceptual object whatsoever as its ground, as the invariant structure of perceptual coherence which *could* be explored *ad infinitum*.

It is thus evident that, though perception gives us the "primary reality," the perceptual world is not the whole of reality for us. It gives me, together with my immediate sense experience, a ground of possibilities, a virtual space which is indefinitely explorable. In this most fundamental sense the world of perception cannot be separated from the world of imagination, since to perceive a world as a *human world* is to perceive it as constituted of possibilities, absences, potentialities, of an indefinite number of other aspects—*implied* in the aspect given to me here and now—which *could* become the objects and themes of future perceptions. There is a "subjunctive" aspect of perceptual experience, and this is the reason why Husserl and Merleau-Ponty say that consciousness, on this primary level of experience, is more of an "I can do" than an "I think that," an invitation to exploration rather than to contemplation.

But over and above the primary prethematic operations of imagination, memory, feeling, etc., which are involved in *any* complete perceptual experience, there are more explicit and deliberate types of imagining and remembering which give us access to regions of reality which have their own consistency, their own temporal and spatial structures, their own "logic," independent of perception. Take, for example, the realms of aesthetic imagination, which we owe chiefly to the work of artists. The world of the Karamazovs created by Dostoevski could serve as an example, but so could the worlds created by a Proust, a Faulkner, a Kafka, a Cézanne, a Beethoven, or a Brahms. We come to live in the world of the Karamazovs only with some difficulty and little by little. It has an ontological status different from that of this mundane world of perceptual consciousness, which we can never really leave while reading Dostoevski or while living in his imaginary world. But as we become acquainted with the characters and temperaments of the sensualist old Fyodor and his atheist son Ivan, as we savor the innocence of Alyosha, the sensuality of Dimitri and, above all, Grushenka, as we begin to see and smell the streets of a nineteenth-century provincial Russian village, and as we penetrate the troubled thoughts of the dying monk Zosima, we gradually enter a different time, a different place, a different moral, social, and spiritual atmosphere from that of our own existence. We may live through the development of a whole generation of Karamazovs in a few hours of our own time. And once we have entered such a world, once we have grasped its distinctive style, its own inner logic, its own necessary laws of development, its own ontological consistency (thanks to which we could never confuse the world of Dostoevski with that of Faulkner, for instance, or either one of them with our own mundane existence), we discover that it, too, is an incomplete world, in which many things could happen in the future or could have happened in the past which we recognize as the specific but unfulfilled possibilities of this story. These possibilities are perfectly determined in the sense that they must be fully consistent with the inner psychology and the inner logic of what has been recorded, but they remain indeterminate invitations to our imagination to complete and fill in the vague and obscure regions whose details have only been sketched.

When we relate such a world of the imagination to the primary world of perception we find that our mode of access to it is determined by very strict laws. Strictly speaking, we cannot *really enter* such a world.[14] We can interrupt it, leave it at will, ignore it, and it is there to be imaginatively re-created and rediscovered *just as we left it*, but without our being able to alter it. It has an ontological consistency, a time and temporal development, a place in history wholly independent of our own mundane existence. There is a sense in which such a world can reveal to us values of truth from which we are cut off in our ordinary real existence. Sometimes such a world appears as *more true* and *more real* than the real world of our perceptual experience. It can be *more true* because it can give us at a glance, so to speak, an essential insight into some aspect of human experience which we ourselves will never experience, never *could* experience, except in imagination. At the same time such a world is wholly built up of the materials of perception, and it is because we can transpose perception into the realm of the imaginary that it can be invented at all. The world of the Karamazovs is perceptually real for the Karamazovs, and while we live in their lives vicariously we are perceiving their world, the rooms of the family villa, the icons on the walls, the borscht and kvass on the table, the socialistic effusions of the journals Ivan has brought with him on the stage from Moscow, etc. Through a fictive manipulation of the perceptual experiences of this, our own ordinary, nondramatic, mundane, perceptual world, we (either of ourselves or following the creative imagination of an artist) are able to transpose the possibilities they offer us to another level of experience and thereby create another world which is nevertheless fully and irrevocably *founded* on this one, though it is not in any sense reducible to it. In this sense the realms of imagination (particularly but not exclusively aesthetic imagination) are higher-order syntheses of thought founded on the primary synthetic activity of perceptual consciousness.

Another example of an order of reality which is founded on perceptual experience but which follows laws different from those which obtain in the real world and which has its own ontological modality is that of memory. There is here, as with imagination, a fundamental prethematic operating activity of memory which is inseparable from perceptual consciousness itself—namely, the primary retentions of consciousness in its ever-flowing temporal stream, thanks to which we experience ourselves to be occupied with stable objects through a given pulse of phenomenal time. It is thanks to this fundamental operating memory that we are able to entertain the *same* thought or the *same* object through a series of psychological processes which are temporally successive to one another. But there is the more explicit and active sense of remembering in which either deliberately or by some accidental association, we relive segments of our past. Some persons are more practiced in this than others, and there are occasions, as for instance the psychiatric interview, when such attempts to "live in the past" are more sustained than they are in everyday life. For instance, if I am now confronted with the task of making some sense of my life which will go beyond the immediate conscious projects of my present situation, I am likely to reflect on patterns of behavior which have recurred at various times in my past experience. The re-creation of the past in this way, and my present experience of it, clearly confronts us with a level of experience essentially different from, and yet necessarily founded on, perceptual experience. When I remember past events or when they intrude upon my consciousness as significant, I do not repeat moment for moment what actually happened during some segment of my past life. I am, in fact, largely incapable of doing this with any accuracy. Certain salient features of past events are organized into patterns, time is telescoped, new typifications and emotional qualities emerge—none of which can claim to have been those I actually experienced at that more or less distant time I am now evoking. And yet it is clear that this is a reordering of "impressions" which at one time were perceptually real for me and that their interest for me lies in their being a restructurization of my *real* perceptual and historical consciousness.

From such orders of reality we could naturally move to the orders of cultural and historical objects, to the order of religious experience, to the objects (constructs, hypotheses, concepts) of the theoretical attitude which is operative in scientific or philosophical research, etc., and ultimately to the level of the most purified idealities (formal or material) of categorial thought. Take, for instance, the cultural institution which is the English language. This is a historical and cultural reality and force of which I am a part and which has formed me and my intellectual processes. It is mine in a very personal sense, since I could not even "think" without it. Yet it is above all a means of intersubjective and historical communication. There was a time, before the fifth century, when it did not exist; moreover, in its diachronic development the phonological, morphological, syntactical, lexicographical systems which constitute it have evolved and are at the present moment undergoing changes. These changes depended and now depend on the effective "usage" of this cultural instrument by all those who in actual fact have spoken and are speaking it, thanks to which its syntax and morphology are at any one time sufficiently fixed (even though they have never been perfectly codified) and its vocabulary sufficiently delimited to distinguish it from other worlds of linguistic expression. We recognize it in the most ungrammatical efforts of children and illiterates and in the harshest accents of foreigners. In what sense can it be said to exist or be experienced by me? Certainly nobody will deny that it is real. It is "wholly" at my disposition when I need to use it, just as it is wholly and entirely at the disposition of all the members of this linguistic community; my peculiar use of it does not inhibit its distinctive use by others. It belongs completely to each and all of us. Yet no one author has exhausted its possibilities, and no one speaker at any given moment can be said to have fully utilized its resources for expression.

The mode of existence of a cultural reality of this kind, dependent on the historical and present linguistic behavior of those who use it, is clearly not the mode of existence of a perceptual object in the primary sense. It exists rather as a kind of cultural space within which I think and speak and write. Its mode of existence is at any given moment more virtual than actual; it offers me an indefinite number of linguistic possibilities among which I choose, without reflection, those I need just now. I perceive it on the lips of others and in the writings of those who have left us books from the past. Clearly it is tied to, and founded on, perception in that its whole reality can be actualized only to the extent that it is an instrument to be used in the real, historical, perceptual world. But it is no less clear that its mode of existence, like that of other intersubjective cultural institutions, is of another order than that of perceptual reality as such, that, though it is tied to time and history, it is endowed in my experience with an atemporal and a nonspatial quality.

Or we could turn to such historical and cultural realities as "feudalism," "capitalism," "Calvinism," "the proletariat," "class warfare," "common law," etc. These are at once historical forces which owe their existence and reality to human action and human intentionality, as well as explanatory hypotheses and concepts. Their mode of reality greatly transcends the real experiences which they thematize and signify, and yet they are clearly founded in the primary mode of consciousness which we call the perceptual world.

It is impossible to give here a complete delineation of the various "orders of reality" and trace out the precise lines of their dependence on the primary structures of perception. At most we can enunciate a thesis to be argued, and it will be convenient to do this in terms of the relationship of categorial thought in general to perception. That such orders of experience as the imaginary, the past, culture, history, etc., are founded in the primary structures of perceptual experience seems evidently less questionable than that the structures of categorial thinking in general are so founded. Moreover, we cannot here do more than allude to the well-known position of Husserl and of Merleau-Ponty and their attempt to avoid the extremes either of "logicism" on the one hand or of "psychologism" on the other in their statements of this thesis.[15] My purpose, thus, is not to present a final demonstration of this thesis but only to investigate its meaning and its claim as it was first stated by William James. This is, therefore, a partial and preparatory study, a restatement of the thesis in Jamesian terms rather than an attempt to establish a definite conclusion.

JAMES'S REFUTATION OF PSYCHOLOGISM

The thesis of the "primacy of perception" in experience can have two senses, and William James anticipated phenomenology in his contribution to the development of each of these. First of all, it can designate the "inescapable" character of the perceptual world and our embodiment within it. On whatever level of conscious awareness we may be operating, our bodily presence to the world continues to be felt and experienced. Even when lost in the worlds of fiction, phenomenal time (i.e., the actual order of our successive acts of imagining) remains the basis of all such other levels of experience, and we continue to grow older even while we advance our scientific and philosophical theories. Even in the most purified realms of theoretical thought, when our physical existence is deliberately bracketed from our consideration, it nevertheless continues to be present in marginal awareness as the inescapable *place* and time in which our thinking takes place. So long as consciousness lives, the perceptual world remains for it its most constant and pervasive realm.

But this is not the most important sense of the thesis of the primacy of perception. There is a stronger sense according to which it is asserted and argued that the perceptual world is not only the necessary (though often more or less marginal) accompaniment of other orders of experience but that the "higher orders" of experience, and more particularly categorial thought, i.e., the realm of (formal and material) ideal meanings, are *founded* on the structures of perception. It is this latter and stronger form of the thesis which we wish to examine with reference to William James.

There is one form of the thesis which must be immediately rejected, and that is *psychologism*, or the belief that the structures of reasoning are to be identified with psychological processes (whether of the individual or of the human historical community as a whole). Husserl's treatment of psychologism is well known, but it is worthwhile reminding ourselves that Husserl himself acknowledged his debt to James's "brilliant observations" in descriptive psychology and credited James's "genius" with helping him learn to avoid the pitfalls of psychologism in his own investigations.[16]

The first level of James's rejection of psychologism is found in his criticism of the "mind-stuff theory" of the British empiricists, particularly Locke and Hume, and his uncovering of the "psychologist's fallacy."[17] As Aron Gurwitsch has claimed of the Gestaltist rejections of the "constancy hypothesis" (i.e., the exclusive and isomorphic dependency of "sense-data" on physical stimuli), James's rejection of the "mind-stuff theory" can be considered to be an implicit phenomeno-logical reduction.[18] James clearly anticipates both Gestalt psychology and the phenomenology of perception in his rejection of atomism or "elementism," i.e., the view that experience is made up of finite, dis-crete, "substantial" bits of color, hardness, softness, thermal qualities, etc. Against such a view, he shows that no psychological act of con-sciousness and no given sensation ever recurs twice, that conscious-ness is "cumulative" and is never twice in identically the same state, and that we cannot construct perception out of the materials of "the perceived."[19] What remains the "same" in a perceptual experience, for instance, are the transcendent "objects" of conscious acts and their meanings, which are fixed by consciousness and stabilized through temporal and synthetic acts which themselves have none of the quali-ties or characters of their objects.

Against such "empiricism" he writes:

> If the thing is composed of parts, then we suppose that the thought of the thing must be composed of the thoughts of the parts. If one part of the thing have appeared in the same thing or in other things on former occa-sions, why then we must be having even now the very same "idea" of that part which was there on those occasions. If the thing is simple, its thought is simple. If it is multitudinous, it must require a multitude of thoughts to think it. If a succession, only a succession of thoughts can know it. If perma-nent, its thought is permanent. And so on *ad libitum*. . . .

> No doubt it is often *convenient* to formulate the mental facts in an atomistic sort of way, and to treat the higher states of consciousness as if they were all built out of unchanging simple ideas. . . .

> But . . . a permanently existing "idea" or "Vorstellung" which makes its appearance before the footlights of consciousness at periodical intervals, is as mythological an entity as the Jack of Spades.[20]

James's contributions to the phenomenological theory of conscious-ness which stem from this criticism of "psychologism" have already been well studied, and it is unnecessary for our purposes to recapitu-late them here.[21]

There is a second level of James's critique of psychologism; he de-veloped it at the end of the *Principles* in the chapter entitled "Neces-sary Truths and the Effects of Experience" in particular reference to John Stuart Mill and Herbert Spencer, who had argued that even the formal structures of categorial thinking could be reduced to psychological processes. Like Husserl in the *Logische Untersuchungen*, which he partially inspired, James utterly rejects this kind of psychologism. James discusses three "ideal" worlds: those of aesthetic, of ethical, and of scientific experience. In all these realms, he says, we experience "ideal and inward relations amongst our objects of thought which can in no intelligible sense whatever be interpreted as reproductions of the order of outer experiences."[22] And it is in the realm of the "forms of judgment"[23] which govern logical necessity that we find the clearest examples of laws of thought which can in no sense be reduced to empirical experience or associative connections. Spencer had argued that even the laws governing logical relationships are the result of "accumulated . . . experiences continued for numberless generations," and can thus be accounted for by the "frequency" with which certain connections have been experienced in the psychological development of the race.[24] Factual investigations of a psychological, anthropological, and physiological character, in short an "evolutionary" epistemology, will uncover the nature of these laws.

In answer to this hypothesis James proposes a purely mental (one might say an "eidetic") experiment:

> Suppose a hundred beings created by God and gifted with the faculties of memory and comparison. Suppose that upon each of them the same lot of sensations are imprinted, but in different orders. Let some of them have no single sensation more than once. Let some have this one and others that one repeated. Let every conceivable permutation prevail. And then let the magic-lantern show die out, and keep the creatures in a void eternity, with naught but their memories to muse upon. Inevitably in their long leisure they will begin to play with the items of their experience and rearrange them, make classificatory series of them, place gray between white and black, orange between red and yellow, and trace all other degrees of resemblance and difference. And this new construction will be absolutely identical in all the hundred creatures, the diversity of the sequence of the original experiences having no effect as regards this rearrangement.
>
> . . . Black will differ from white just as much in a world in which they always come close together as in one in which they always come far apart; just as much in one in which they appear rarely as in one in which they appear all the time.
>
> To learn whether black and white differ I need not consult the world of experience at all; the mere ideas suffice. *What I mean* by black differs from *what I mean* by white, whether such colors exist *extra mentem mean* or not.[25]

What James discovers in this "free imaginary variation" is the "ideal law" which governs judgments of comparison, and he sees that it functions independently of associative experience on the perceptual level. If we could, *per impossibile*, be restricted to the phenomenal materials which spontaneously offer themselves in temporal continuity and succession to perceptual consciousness, it would be utterly impossible for consciousness to conceive of any general law at all. "From the point of view of strict empiricism nothing exists but the sum of particular perceptions with their coincidences on the one hand, their contradictions on the other."[26] The "sense" or "meaning" of sameness and difference is experienced in another way than the temporally ordered objects of perceptual experience. There is a realm of experience, to which judgments of comparison belong, which is not subject to the conditions of perception. Such judgments of categorial thought have an a-temporal and a-spatial quality of a very special kind, which we can call "ideal." James goes on, then, to examine this "large body of *a priori*, or intuitively necessary truths"[27] which are implied in systematic classification, logical inference, subsumption, etc. Such "truths" are experienced as endowed with a universal validity for which no "mere outgrowth of habit and association" could account.[28] They are "necessary and eternal relations" which "form a determinate system, independent of the order of frequency in which experience may have associated their originals in time and space."[29]

The Ideal and the Perceptual

Thus James vindicates the distinction between categorial thought and perceptual consciousness and asserts that the structure of relationships which he calls "laws of logic" or the "forms of judgment" have a mode of reality independent of psychological processes (whether of the individual or of the race as a whole). He has, therefore, escaped *psychologism*. It is also certain that nobody has ever accused him of logicism or Platonism on the other side. St. Augustine had argued that in such purely conceptual realms as those of logic, mathematics, ethics, etc., the experience of eternal truth proves that there is a kind of knowing which gives us an object *superior* to our perceptual faculties and our embodied intellects, and he went on to prove, on this basis, that God is the necessary foundation of such superior truths. In short, according to Augustine and the Platonists, we have two radically distinct faculties directed toward radically distinct kinds of objects (and there is only an indirect, ontological connection between them). The traditional affirmation of the superiority of pure intellectual intuition over sense intuition, and of the "separateness" of its object from the data of sense, remained intact through Leibniz and the early Kant. With his elaboration of the *apriori* forms of space and time, Kant discovered a kind of object of knowledge intermediary between intellectual intuition and sense intuition—namely, the universal and necessary forms under which sensibility synthesizes everything presented to it. Husserl continued this development by arguing that there are not two radically different kinds of objects of knowledge but rather that intellectual (or categorial) intuition and perceptual intuition are two different ways of having the *same objects,* that these two levels of intuition are inseparable and coordinate means of objectifying the world. It is easy to situate James in this historical development, even though he himself is unaware of it. He does not at any point recognize a superior "intellectual intuition" as a function of the mind utterly separate from its other powers of cognition, which could commune with "necessary truth" outside the whole tissue of factual, empirical experience. Like Husserl, he would argue that necessary truths are "of perception," that they are inseparably given together with primary, perceptual reality. He argues always that we experience "feelings" of *and,* of *if,* of *but,* and of *by* as surely as we do feelings of *blue* or *cold.* When he says, for instance, that "the inmost nature of reality is congenial to our powers," he is making a statement on reality and a statement on knowing; the world we perceive and the world we think are the same world, and logic and perception play into one another's hands. He would agree with Albert Einstein that "the eternal mystery of the world is its comprehensibility." His problem is to unite what is given in experience as inseparably conjoined (both in the subject and in the object) and yet distinct: perception and thought.[30]

Our final question here, then, will be to ask how James conceives the interrelations which obtain within experience between the ideal order of categorial thought and the real order of perceptual reality. Should we say, as we would of Husserl and Merleau-Ponty, that the categorial order is *founded on,* though certainly irreducible to, the perceptual?

That the ideal orders of number systems, of mathematics, of logical laws (whether formal or "transcendental") constitute an autonomous order of experience, distinct from the perspectivity, the phenomenal time and phenomenal space which characterize perception, is clear.[31] But this is also the case for any eidetically distinct domain of consciousness, of the imaginary, of memory, of cultural objects, of the theoretical constructs of science, etc. The question is, rather, how we should view these peculiarly ideal operations of consciousness which we encounter in categorial thought. The empiricist tradition, in its psychologistic form, has attempted to reduce them to perception; the idealistic and logicist tradition has attempted to locate them in the spiritual realm and to postulate a special spiritual power in man, distinct from his ordinary powers of consciousness, to account for our experience of them. The phenomenologists have attempted to show that, though consciousness can live in different orders of reality, all these realms are interrelated and ultimately grounded in perception, that reasoning and judgment are implied in the prereflexive experiences of perceptual consciousness, and that the ideal of "truth" is given implicitly in the least perception.

As Merleau-Ponty has stated it:

> By these words, the "primacy of perception," we mean that the experience of perception is our presence at the moment when things, truths, values are constituted for us; that perception is a nascent *logos*; that it teaches us . . . the true conditions of objectivity itself; that it summons us to the tasks of knowledge and action. It is not a question of reducing human knowledge to sensation, but of assisting at the birth of this knowledge, to make it as sensible as the sensible, to recover the consciousness of rationality.[32]

Like Merleau-Ponty, James centers his studies on the phenomenon of "rationality" rather than on a hypostatized and static *reason*. In his study of thinking and reasoning James particularly insists on the teleological and "practical" character of the structures of classification, analogy, and definition we employ. He calls them "teleological weapons of the mind."[33] Meaning and essence, as they emerge in thought, are determined by my active interest in the objects I am dealing with.

> All ways of conceiving a concrete fact, if they are true ways at all, are equally true ways. *There is no property absolutely essential to any one thing.* The same property which figures as the essence of a thing on one occasion becomes a very inessential feature upon another. Now that I am writing, it is essential that I conceive my paper as a surface for inscription. If I failed to do that, I should have to stop my work. But if I wished to light a fire . . . the essential way of conceiving the paper would be as combustible material. . . . It is really *all* that it is: a combustible, a writing surface, a thin thing, a hydrocarbonaceous thing, a thing eight inches

one way and ten another, a thing just one furlong east of a certain stone in my neighbor's field, an American thing, etc., etc., *ad infinitum*. Whichever one of these aspects of its being I temporarily class it under, makes me unjust to the other aspects. But as I am always classing it under one aspect or another, I am always unjust, always partial, always exclusive. My excuse is necessity—the necessity which my finite and practical nature lays upon me. My thinking is first and last and always for the sake of my doing, and I can only do one thing at a time.[34]

But someone may urge, this may be all very well and good for the empirical and practical meanings (or essences) by means of which we constitute and order the immediate chaos of perceptual experience, but what of the more formal aspects of categorial thought? How do these relate to such practical experience? While it is true that James does not advance any explicit theory on this subject, he was throughout his life interested in the interrelations between "theoretical" and "practical" thinking. James recognized two kinds of truth: *a priori* truths (which are "of thinking") and *a posteriori* truths (which are "of experience"). He attempted to coordinate and interrelate these two kinds of truth by giving the primacy to truths "of experience." Thinking and perceiving are two hierarchically ordered and coordinated ways of dealing with the same reality.[35]

Reality, as it exists, is a *plenum*. "All its parts are contemporaneous, each is as real as any other, and each as essential for making the whole just what it is and nothing else."[36] But *as we experience and think* reality, this *plenum* (which is itself neither experienceable nor thinkable as such) takes on the diverse qualities of perceptual organization, of invitations to our imagination and our affections, of objects of our theoretical and scientific interest.

> The world as it is given at this moment is the sum total of all its beings and events now. But can we think of such a sum? . . . we break it: we break it into histories, and we break it into arts, and we break it into sciences; and then we begin to feel at home. We make ten thousand separate serial orders of it. On any one of these, we may react as if the rest did not exist. We discover among its parts relations that were never given to sense at all—mathematical relations, tangents, squares, and roots and logarithmic functions—and out of an infinite number of these we call certain ones essential and lawgiving, and ignore the rest. Essential these relations are, but only *for our purpose,* the other relations being just as real and present as they; and our purpose is to *conceive simply* and to *foresee*.[37]

James likes to show that the theoretical constructions of categorial thought—far from being eternal and nonhistorical ideas in the mind of God or the impersonal order which could be conceived only by a universal thinker, who could view the whole of reality in all its interrelated aspects from every point of view and from no point of view in particular, as James says, "without emphasis,"—are rather progressively elaborated and precarious "instruments" or "weapons" men have forged in order to think the real.

There are many possible constructions of purely theoretical reason, in which logical relations might obtain, and be recognized as valid, but which could be of no conceivable use to human thought. We must, therefore, attempt to understand, says James, why it is that our very peculiar world, the life-world of immediate experience, "plays right into logic's hands"[38] We are able, in fact, to think the world of objects within which we live according to abstract formal laws of relationships, which constitute, in themselves, a "fixed system," particularly congenial to our intellects but without apparent and immediate justification within the empirical order of phenomenal time and space. In his studies on rationality and belief James shows that it is a "postulate of rationality" itself that the world *be* rationally intelligible on the pattern of *some* ideal system.

> The whole war of the philosophies is over that point of faith. Some say they can see their way already to the rationality; others that it is hopeless. . . . One philosopher at least says that the relatedness of things to each other is irrational . . . and that a world of relations can never be made intelligible.[39]

James is not such a philosopher. He argues for a view which would render justice to the "truths of reason," to the formal laws of thought, while at the same time believing that the manifold structures of consciousness are a unified, overlapping, and interconnecting texture. The unity of thought and perception is ultimately founded on our experience that the world we think is the same world as that in which we are immersed by perception and which is the correlate of our active and practical interests. The laws of logical relationships are in fact discovered again in the internal and external "relations" of perceptual experience, and it is for this reason that they are "applicable" to it. Perceptual consciousness and categorial thought are not totally separate "faculties," without interconnections, but in our experience itself they play continually into one another's hands. Ultimately, we would have to ask whether the world we perceive would be the same world it is if it were not constituted by a consciousness capable of thinking it as well as imagining it and, conversely, whether the structures of categorial thought could exist for us at all except as instruments implied by the world of perception for use within that world. If we state the question in this way, there is no doubt where James stands in "the war of the philosophies."

But, in conclusion, can we give a clear and final assessment of James's contribution to this problem? In a symposium dedicated to William James *and* phenomenology there is a double danger: of minimizing his contributions as accidental stumblings onto "truths" which only the full-fledged phenomenology of Husserl can justify or, conversely, of maximizing James into a phenomenologist in the contemporary sense of the term. With the Yankee honesty which should characterize any treatment of James's texts, I think it is necessary to conclude that, on this problem at least, James remains a precursor—but a *genuine* precursor. As is frequently the case in James, his problematic is more interesting than his systematic conclusions. He gives a clear, provocative, and contemporary statement of the problem. There is no doubt as to the thesis he holds or as to the direction in which research must be initiated to discover the solution. But he left it to his progeny to work out the arguments and the demonstrations. It is at once in the unfinished nature of his reflections and in what we see to be their continuation and completion in Husserl and Merleau-Ponty, that we find our right and our duty to continue the discussions we have begun here.

II William James and Phenomenology

Ever since the death of William James there has been a disposition on the part of his American followers to take a very possessive, even chauvinistic, view of his philosophy, as if its significance were somehow bound up with some intention (whether explicit or unexpressed) to exemplify a stage of the national self-consciousness.[1] Within a year of James's death Josiah Royce eulogized his ability to give expression to ideas "which are characteristic of a stage and an aspect of the spiritual life of this people,"[2] and his major biographers and commentators have emphasized the New-Worldly practicality, the pluralistic open-endedness, the restless frontiersmanship of his Yankee style, congenitally hostile to the empty rationalisms and idealisms of Old Europe. We all find this to be most congenial and, to a certain extent, it is true. James not only was, but recognized himself to be, the very antithesis of a systematic German *Gelehrter*, and his comments on the likes of Kant, Hegel, Meinong, and others betray not only opposition to their systematic thought but considerable malicious pleasure in being able to deflate the pedantry and "humbug" of their language and their *strengwissenschaftlich* pretensions. Meinong is the "unspeakable Meinong"—not only for the complexities and intricacies of his doctrine of "supposals" and *Objektive*, but because of his "complacent *Breite*."[3] James's praise of Wundt ("Was there ever, since Christian Wolff's time, such a model of the German Professor?") is double-edged: "He isn't a genius, he is a *professor*—a being whose duty is to know everything, and have his opinion about everything connected with his *Fach*. . . ."[4] As Wilshire observes, James "seems to relish nothing more than a chance to attack Kant,"[5] and, we might add, "his unhappy legacy."[6]

With Kant, complication both of thought and statement was an inborn infirmity, enhanced by the musty academicism of his Konigsburg existence. With Hegel it was a raging fever. Terribly, therefore, do the sour grapes which these fathers of philosophy have eaten set our teeth on edge. (I, 365–66)[7]

Certainly we are justified in saying that William James did not find his principal philosophical inspiration in meditating on the style or content of German idealism or transcendental philosophy in any form known to him, and the man who in his letters continually refers to his self-imposed mission to "fight Hegel" can only with irony be now accused of practicing "phenomenology"—a *term* he would probably have loathed. Therefore, those who would now attempt to incorporate his thought into the framework of European, and particularly Husserlian, phenomenology are—in the face of the officially authorized version of James's philosophy—going to have to make a case. But there *are* ironies in the history of philosophy and the one which operates within the link which we are now, I believe, forced to recognize between the names of James and Husserl is one of the most instructive. The literature on William James and phenomenology has grown during the past few years into a corpus of sufficient size and intrinsic philosophical interest to require that it no longer be ignored.[8] Even interpreters of James who wish to remain wholly within the "American" tradition of philosophy, loyal to the authorized version of his thought and free from contamination by foreign accents and strange philosophical ways, have begun to recognize the peculiar impetus provided to the present James renaissance by the discovery of his importance for Husserl. William James Earle, in a recent article meant apparently to summarize the present status of philosophical work on James (since it appears in *The Encyclopedia of Philosophy* of 1967), remains faithful, it is true, to the traditional provincialism,[9] but John J. McDermott, in his equally recent edition of *The Writings of William James*, recognizes the "promise"[10] of this new literature for a philosophical re-evaluation of James's thought in the light of contemporary philosophical concerns, even though he himself remains outside it.

Of course, about historical influences or their importance for philosophy one cannot decide by fiat, but only by turning to the evidence, *zu den Sachen selbst*, in the historical record itself. Thus there will be many who will not simply believe because William James Earle says so that "the main philosophical significance of [James's]

Principles" lies uniquely in its historical influence on the "subsequent movement in philosophy typified by Whitehead and his disciples."[11] They will, perhaps, not question in any way the great importance of James for Whitehead (which is, in any case, undeniable and well documented both historically and in the solid philosophical achievements of this school of thought), but they will point out that other philosophers besides Whitehead read James. Among these was one whom a few would also rank among the "greats" of the twentieth century, namely, Edmund Husserl.

The salient facts of this influence are well established in the literature being considered here; there is no longer any doubt or obscurity concerning the historical record, and historians of philosophy are henceforth permitted to ignore it only if, after examining the evidence, they conclude that this influence was marginal or of no philosophical importance. I believe that these recent studies show beyond doubt that the relationship between the thought of James and Husserl, and likewise between the thought of James and some later existential phenomenologists, is of great philosophical significance not only for a correct assessment of the impact of these various philosophical developments up to now but also for the continuing philosophical work of elaborating and refining an adequate and self-critical phenomenology in the future. It is certainly not my view, or a conclusion supported by this literature, that William James merely stumbled by accident upon a number of "truths" about the structure of experience which can now be adequately accounted for only by "correcting" them (as Aquinas "corrected" Aristotle) and placing them within the strict confines of some supposedly orthodox transcendental idealism. In many cases James preceded and certainly developed what were to become essential phenomenological themes prior to, and independently of, the work of European phenomenologists. These ideas, which lead to pragmatism, radical empiricism, pluralism, the philosophies of Whitehead and Dewey, must continue to be examined and developed in the directions which logically flow from them even independently of their convergence with phenomenology. In short, the value of James's thought as a whole is not exhausted in its importance for phenomenology in any narrow sense. At the same time the phenomenologists' interest in James, if it is to be genuine, cannot be one of a mere tactic, an attempt to find American respectability for its program by producing a set of suitable "quotes" from James's diversified corpus. An external and purely factitious agreement of this kind would be without interest or value to anyone.[12] It is only because of the intrinsic and logically necessary convergences within James's philosophical discoveries and those of the phenomenologists that we can show that they make contributions to what is, in essential respects, the same program; that they hold fundamental doctrines in common; and that these doctrines are thus intrinsically and necessarily fated to the same philosophical triumph or failure. This is not to claim a *total* convergence between James and phenomenology, or to deny ourselves the right to correct the one by the other, or to criticize, approve, or reject both together, or separately, for weaknesses and errors which have become or may become apparent as these ideas are developed. It is, rather, to claim that within William James there is an authentic "phenomenologist" in the strict sense of the term, that his thought went through an authentic phenomenological development (though this was never his exclusive concern), that the similarities between his thought and that of a Husserl and a Merleau-Ponty are not fortuitous and external but that they stem from certain fundamental discoveries, options, and positions which logically implicate them, together, in a common philosophical endeavor.

William James was accorded even in his own lifetime extraordinary respect on the part of European (and, earliest of all, German) philosophers, and Santayana was perfectly correct in noting that "until the return wave of James' reputation reached America from Europe, his pupils and friends were hardly aware that he was such a distinguished man."[13] This interest and respect was, frequently enough, not reciprocated and, at least in the case of Husserl and phenomenology, we have to say that James's influence was unidirectional. He came to influence Husserl quite profoundly, but this passed almost unbeknownst to James and we know of no direct reciprocal influence of Husserl on James. This was in large part because of the disparity in their ages and the fact that Husserl's first major treatise to employ James's ideas, *Logische Untersuchungen*, was published only in 1900 and 1901, after James's thought had matured and his contacts with German philosophy were no longer as open as they had been in his youth. Carl Stumpf, fellow disciple of Brentano and colleague at Halle to whom Husserl dedicated the *Logische Untersuchungen*, had met James in Prague in 1882 and became, thereafter, James's closest friend and most constant correspondent in the German academic world. There is no doubt that it was Stumpf who got his younger colleague, Husserl, interested in James's *Principles of Psychology* ("the best of all psychologies").[14] But so far as we can tell he failed in any attempt to get James interested in Husserl. In fact it was James himself who, some years later, advised a great eastern publishing house in America against publishing a translation of *Logische Untersuchungen* ("Nobody in America would be interested in a new and strange German work on Logic") to Husserl's lasting grief and, it must be said, to the detriment of American philosophy.[15] This major contribution to twentieth-century philosophy has now finally appeared in an English translation by J. N. Findlay but, if it had been available to English-speaking philosophers at the turn of the century, it is possible that they would not have had to first learn from Europeans of James's distinctive contribution to what, after the Second World War, was to develop into the dominant current of thought in Western Europe. More than once, therefore, it has fallen to European philosophers to instruct us on the importance and originality of certain facets of James's thought which had gone unperceived on these shores.

It is unnecessary to repeat here the whole historical record; this can be examined in detail in the work provided by Spiegelberg, Linschoten, and others. It is sufficient here to recapitulate a few salient facts. Husserl's library, preserved at Louvain, contains most of James's major works and two reprints James sent to Husserl. Only the *Principles of Psychology,* however, and one of the reprints, "The Knowing of Things Together," contain marks and marginal notes which indicate that they were read intensively.[16] In the diary, written during his period of crisis in 1906, Husserl tells us that he first read the *Principles* in 1891 and 1892 in connection with a course he was giving on descriptive psychology[17] and in an article published in 1894 he first explicitly cites the work of James in a discussion of the objective contents of acts of consciousness.[18] As is well known he credits James, in *Logische Untersuchungen,*[19] with teaching him how to overcome psychologism, and, in *Krisis,*[20] with being the first to describe the horizonal structure of experience in his notion of the "fringes of consciousness." Husserl's recognition of a debt to James is thus completely explicit; he calls him "a daring and original man," an "excellent investigator," unshackled by any tradition, a "genius," and states in his diary that James's influence was important for his own work.[21]

It will be noticed from Husserl's references to James and from a glance at the literature of interpretation these references have evoked that, up to now at any rate, phenomenological interest in James's work has been centered on the works being *Principles of Psychology* rather than on his later works. The books referred to here deal almost exclusively with themes found in the *Principles*. Wilshire explicitly

subtitles his work a "Study of the *Principles of Psychology*."[22]
Linschoten uses James's later writings only to the extent that they extend and illustrate the development of positions already taken in the *Principles* and any discussion of his later theories is marginal to his main purpose, namely to show that "James repeatedly paved the way for a phenomenological psychology, although it must be said that sometimes he blocked it again."[23] Only the book by John Wild exhibits a more systematic attempt to cover the whole of James's work but, even here, ten chapters out of fifteen are devoted to summarizing and commenting on the *Principles*.[24]

In this sense Wild's treatment of James represents a new departure and shows that two things can and now should be done by the phenomenological commentators on James, (1) to show that there is at least *some* implicit system in James's thought which unites the themes he developed in his later writings with the more explicitly phenomenological themes which appear in the *Principles* and (2), on this basis, to give a phenomenological critique of his later formulations of pragmatism, the pragmatic theory of truth, pluralism, and radical empiricism. I shall return to this at the end of this study. But it is not at all unfortunate that the phenomenologists have, up to now, put the *Principles* at the center of their attention. This is James's one completed and only truly systematic treatise.[25] It lays the groundwork for all his later more popular essays and lectures and is by all accounts his *chef d'oeuvre*.[26] Though it is his first major work, it is no youthful production. It was twelve years in the writing and was published when James had reached the age of forty-nine, after years of teaching, writing, and empirical research.[27] It is moreover the work which has been least studied by James's American successors, the book which in the whole of his corpus deserves and needs the greatest amount of clarification, commentary, and discussion.[28] The recent phenomenological interpretations of sections of this work are transforming our understanding of James and should lead to the discovery of a number of new and important directions for philosophical and psychological research. Let us examine more closely, now, some of the discoveries which have been made.

THE INTENTIONAL THEORY OF CONSCIOUSNESS

Coming after the work already accomplished by Gurwitsch and Linschoten, Bruce Wilshire has produced what is probably the best commentary on the *Principles* which has yet been written. It is cogently and economically argued, skillfully arranged around one central strand in James's work, namely, the "phenomenological breakthrough" accomplished by James's discovery of the law of the intentionality of consciousness—and this in spite of the manifest intent of his psychological program and without his ever coming to a full understanding of the implications of what he had established. The full-fledged and fully explicit elaboration of the notion of intentionality was accomplished only by Husserl (on the basis, in part, of James's work) but there is no doubt, as Husserl recognized in the *Krisis*, that James had in his theory of consciousness all the materials necessary to effect the "transcendental turn." Intentionality can be taken in a weak and commonsensical sense, namely, that all consciousness is consciousness *of* something, that consciousness is world-directed, and deals with entities or "objects" transcendent to itself. This first sense of the notion of intentionality is one found in the Greeks, in the Scholastics, in Brentano, and owes nothing specific to phenomenology. There have been very few philosophers in history who have not known this much, and they have used it as the commonsensical basis for separating knowing subjects and acts of consciousness, on the one hand, from objects known and cognized, on the other. Even so, we might grant to Husserl that intentionality even in this weak sense is a law of experience which never was and never could have been discovered by empirical psychology since it involves an eidetic analysis of *what is meant* by consciousness and is a "transcendental" structure of experience whose validity is neither confirmed nor infirmed by empirical procedures which must always already take it for granted. It is of the "essence" of consciousness that it "deal with objects independent of itself" (in the words of James),[29] i.e., that it is a "cognitive" or "presentational" process.

This is what led Brentano, on the basis of the Scholastic theories of "intentional existence," to distinguish conscious processes from all other kinds of processes as ways of "having objects," and James, like Husserl, refers to the work of Brentano when he takes up this problem.[30] But, as Herbert Spiegelberg was, I believe, the first to point out, there is more to James's theory of intentionality than this; he went beyond Brentano's description of intentionality to show that (1) it involves the identification and objectification of "objects" which can be *identically the same* for a multiplicity of different acts of consciousness, and that (2) it is an active and selective achievement of consciousness rather than a merely passive or static directedness to objects already constituted in their specificity independent of the acts which grasp them as "objects."[31] This all sounds very Husserlian and it is. It is very likely that Husserl did not find the unique source of his theory of intentionality in James and that the specifically phenomenological and "strong" sense of the law of intentionality has roots in his earliest philosophical reflections on and reactions to Brentano,[32] but it is striking nevertheless that it is these very additions to Brentano's minimal conception of intentionality which figure in the passages of the *Principles* most carefully studied by Husserl.

We will do our best, now, to recapitulate briefly Wilshire's account which is the most complete and systematic (and dramatic!) analysis of how James came upon this discovery.

At the beginning of the *Principles* James describes his program for a "natural scientific psychology" as "a thoroughgoing dualism."

> Psychology . . . assumes as its data (1) *thoughts and feelings*, and (2) *a physical world* in time and space with which they coexist and which (3) *they know*. Of course these data themselves are discussable; but the discussion of them (as of other elements) is called metaphysics and falls outside the province of this book. This book, assuming that thoughts and feelings exist and are vehicles of knowledge, thereupon contends that psychology when she has ascertained the empirical correlation of the various sorts of thought or feeling with definite conditions of the brain, can go no farther, that is, as a natural science. If she goes farther she becomes metaphysical.[33]

James's "manifest program" in the *Principles* is, therefore, the establishment of a science of mental life by correlating "its phenomena and their conditions" (I,l). The *phenomena* are feelings, desires, cognitions, reasonings, decisions, and so on; they are "mental states" (for which James interchangeably uses words like "thought" and "feeling"). Their causal conditions are physiological events, primarily states of the brain. It is hypothetically possible, James assumes, to correlate "mental states" with "brain states" in such a way as to give a purely objective and scientific explanation of how the former are conditioned by the latter without invoking any "metaphysics." There are "thoughts," "things known," and a causal link between the two. It is the causal link which psychology studies. What could be more clear or more obvious?

But this "manifest program," which is invoked again at several later stages in the development of the *Principles*, each time with decreasing confidence, is, in the end, abandoned, though James himself seems somewhat mystified and confused as to just why it broke down.

In the last chapter of the *Briefer Course* he admits that his "scientific psychology" has become one into which "the waters of metaphysical criticism leak at every joint."[34] His methodological dualism involved assumptions which could not be left uncriticized after all.

> From the common-sense point of view (which is that of all the natural sciences) knowledge is an ultimate relation between two mutually external entities, the knower and the known. The world first exists, and then the states of the mind; and these gain a cognizance of the world which gets gradually more complete. But it is hard to carry through this simple dualism, *for idealistic reflections intrude.*[35]

In order to correlate brain states and mental states, we have to be able to specify what each is. But, unfortunately for his dualistic program, it is impossible to specify what a "mental state" *is* merely on the basis of its being externally and causally conditioned by something outside it (and this is why James's supposed hesitancies between interactionism, parallelism, epiphenomenalism, or his "comminuted *Identitätsphilosophie*" are all ultimately irrelevant). What does his "scientific" psychology finally come to?

> A string of raw facts; a little gossip and wrangle about opinions; a little classification and generalization on the mere descriptive level; a strong prejudice that we *have* states of mind, and that our brain conditions them: but not a single law. . . . This is no science, it is only the hope of a science.[36]

But there is, of course, more to James's psychology than this poignant admission of failure on the last page. There is, above all, his "metaphysics." He began by saying that a properly scientific study of the mind would eschew all metaphysics, but he was unable to maintain this program even through the first chapter of his book (as Wilshire admirably shows); by chapter five he is freely mingling "metaphysics" and "science," and by chapter six he has become "exclusively metaphysical."

> Metaphysics [he now writes] means nothing but an unusually obstinate effort to think clearly. The fundamental conceptions of psychology are practically very clear to us, but theoretically they are very confused, and one easily makes the obscurest assumptions in this science without realizing until challenged, what internal difficulties they involve. (I, 145)

What James is struggling with here is the "thoroughgoing dualism" of mental states and their external causes with which he so confidently began. But the assumptions which underlie such a methodological dualism necessarily involve him in *erkenntnistheoretische* considerations or "metaphysics" understood as a criticism of his assumptions,[37] and James finds that he can make no progress along the line of what was to be the major, announced direction of his research without doing something else first. It is at this point that he begins to distinguish the phenomenological from the physiological levels of investigation. Little by little he abandons the latter (which he now terms his "physiological preliminaries")[38] and gets down to the philosophical analysis of knowledge. But because he nevertheless continues to speak these two very different languages (of the theory of meaning on the one hand and of the causal conditions of thought on the other) haphazardly throughout the rest of the text, Wilshire considers the book seriously "flawed."

> James can never really get started in his natural scientific program, and . . . he must always do something else before he can do what he planned to do next. It is as if he started a race at the middle and could get to the starting line only by going back over the track he wants to run. But he seems to be in doubt as to where the starting line might be, so he runs backward in order to keep the goal always in view. Of course, he cannot see clearly where he is going, but he is making an amazing effort to locate the starting line. . . . Repeatedly we observe James's strange mode of progression in the *Principles:* he cannot sustain his forward pace because he must always go back to uncover the foundation of his own presuppositions. He gets ahead of himself; but ahead of himself in an odd kind of way: he cannot run backward fast enough to keep up with himself.[39]

James was the first to launch the notion that consciousness is a temporally flowing "stream" of experiences which continually change, grow, and merge with one another,[40] and he believed, at first, that one could grasp these mental acts (or "feelings" or "thoughts") by "introspection" and then correlate them with their "causes." But every time he tried to grasp such a mental act the only thing he could fix clearly in mind was *its object*. He discovered that no mental act could be specified except through its object and, then, he shifted his ground from an introspective analysis of the stream of thought to an analysis of "thought's object."[41] Thought, he found, was not something which could be isolated or studied independently of its cognitive or presentational function; he found that "thought" *is* intrinsically and necessarily a cognitive relationship, that what we *mean* by "mind" and mental acts is our ability to fix and cognize the same object of thought through different mental acts which are temporally distinct from one another.

Let us agree, commonsensically, that there is an external cause of the thought (or sensation, or feeling) I am experiencing, that this external event is a necessary condition of my having my thought of it. It nevertheless remains that unless I know, over and above the fact *that* I am experiencing something, *what kind of thing is meant* in this experience of it, I cannot specify it as a thought; otherwise, I would never know what to look for as the "cause" of my experience. The determination of meaning, as Wilshire happily puts it, is logically prior to the determination of truth (p. 27), and a thought can be specified only in terms of what it is *of*. This specification is independent of all questions of truth or verification and this is why James uses the term "cognition" (which is the fundamental and "omnipresent" characteristic of conscious experience)[42] in a generic sense. He distinguishes "successful cognition" (truth) from "unsuccessful cognition" (error). Physiological psychology may be able to account for "unsuccessful cognition" (e.g., the patient fails to perceive the nurse because he is chloroformed) but something more than this kind of physiological explanation is necessary to account for "successful cognition." There is a radical difference between causal conditions and logical conditions, and unless we know what a cognition *means* or intends, what is is *of*, we cannot ever determine what the conditions of its success or failure would be.

James, then, discovers the intentionality of consciousness. Thought, he says, is primarily a selective objectification directed toward "ends." What is immediately presented is not the mental state itself but its object.

> Does not the same piano-key, struck with the same force, make us hear in the same way? Does not the same grass give us the same feeling of green . . . ? It seems a piece of metaphysical sophistry to suggest that we do not; and yet a close attention to the matter shows that *there is no proof that the same sensation is ever got by us twice. What is got twice is the same OBJECT*. (I, 231)

A nerve current in the organism is a particular, datable event. If every sensation or thought were strictly correlated with an individual nerve current, each would be as distinguishable, individual, and separate as these physiological events and we would never know whether we could be thinking of the same thing in two successive acts of consciousness. But this is not our experience.

> Each conception . . . eternally remains what it is, and never can become another. The mind may change its states, and its meanings, at different times; may drop one conception and take up another, but the dropped conception can in no intelligible sense be said to *change into* its successor. The paper, a moment ago white, I may now see to have been scorched black. But my conception "white" does not change into my conception "black." On the contrary, it stays alongside of the objective blackness as a different meaning in my mind, and by so doing lets me judge the blackness as the paper's change. Unless it stayed, I should simply say "blackness" and know no more. Thus, amid the flux of opinions and physical things, the world of conceptions, or things intended to be thought about, stands stiff and immutable, like Plato's Realm of Ideas. (I, 462)

> Even now, the world may be a place in which the same thing never did and never will come twice. The thing we mean to point at may change from top to bottom and we be ignorant of the fact. But in our meaning itself we are not deceived; our intention is to think of the same. (I, 460)

What the "physiological preliminaries" cannot account for is the mind's "sense of the same." This sense of sameness is "the keel of the mind" and things can be *the same* only for a mind which can grasp them and hold them before itself through the flux of temporal experience.[43] But minds, as ever moving streams of conscious acts which flow in upon one another, are also in some sense forever changing. Thus "the sense of the same" through which objects are constituted for consciousness is an achievement of consciousness which can no more be reduced to mental states than it can be reduced to physical states both of which are, at the bare minimum, temporally juxtaposed and different from one another. Thus, neither physiological studies nor "introspection" is sufficient to account for the structure of our mental life; what is necessary is intentional or meaning-analysis of the *object of thought* as it is given presentationally in experience. James, Wilshire shows, provides all the elements necessary for such an analysis. He distinguishes the *object of thought* from the act of consciousness in which it is given, and he likewise distinguishes it from the objective referent (which he terms the "topic" of a thought) towards which it is directed and which would "verify" it. Let us take these up in turn.

First of all, there is a necessary and internal relationship between a thought (in the sense of a process of thinking or experiencing) and this thought's *object*. This is not a fortuitous or empirical relation but a question of the logical conditions of the meaning of this thought. The thought cannot be specified in any other way than by stating what it is *of,* by its *object*. Or, to put it in Wilshire's words:

> The point of a transcendental investigation is to expose necessary truths which must be presupposed if that which is actual (e.g., in the way of phenomena) is to be shown to be possible, that is, intelligible. For phenomenology a fundamental presupposition is the necessary truth which expresses the cognitive relationship: the very concept of a mental state involves the concept of its object; without this presupposition neither term in the relationship is intelligible. This is the doctrine of intentionality. (p. 17)

James, who began as an empirical scientist, was led by the examination of his presuppositions to the statement of an apriori (or transcendental) law, i.e., a condition of the *meaning* of the phenomenon in question, in a similar manner. He found that there is no possibility of there being consciousness except as *consciousness of objects* because that is what consciousness means, and it is necessarily and forever impossible to distinguish or designate an act of consciousness except through a specification of its *object*. That James, in the *Principles*, stated this law of intentionality in a way which goes beyond that found by Brentano in the Scholastics, and, in effect, includes the specific characteristics of intentionality as they were developed by Husserl seems beyond doubt. That he had, however, only an imperfect awareness that he had done so is scarcely less doubtful. That is why we are required to say both that he effected the transcendental turn (in Husserl's sense) and that he remained "on the way toward a phenomenological psychology"—an initiator and explorer who did not himself enter the promised land he had discovered.[44]

But James went further than establishing the internal logical relationship of an act of consciousness to its meaning ("the thought *just as it thinks it*"); he made solid contributions to mapping out and delineating the field of consciousness in many of its details—we will discuss some of these shortly. He was the first to distinguish between the "field" of a given meaning and its "margins." And, above all, he distinguished the "object" of thought in the strict sense (its meaning) from the "topic" (or referent in the real world) which it is "about."[45] This was elaborated more fully in his distinction between "knowledge by acquaintance" and "knowledge about" something. Every "object" of thought bears within itself a reference to its possible instantiation in actual experience; "knowledge about" things (or the cognition of meanings) terminates in acts of direct sensory "acquaintance" (or the cognition of truth and verification) which may or may not be fulfilled but which, in "successful cognition," prescribe the ultimate epistemic conditions of valid knowledge. In other words, both "knowledge about" and "knowledge by acquaintance" are directed toward the life-world as a whole and it is this life-world itself, as the "horizon" of any particular cognition, which is the final a priori ground of all experience. The structures of the mind are therefore not distinct from the structures of the life-world but can be known only through the description of this world as it is experienced and "lived" prior to reflection on the mental processes themselves. This thesis in James comes to an incipient and implicit phenomenological reduction and is, no doubt, what he means by the "idealistic reflections" which kept intruding upon him and impeded his attempt to give an explanation of knowledge in terms of physiology and science, since physiology and science themselves are possible only within the life-world as special and restricted systems of explanation of what is primordially given. As Wilshire puts it very well, if a knowledge of physiology and of the physiological conditions of life-world experience were necessary to understand perception, Aristotle, for instance, who believed that the brain was merely an organ for cooling the blood, would have nothing to tell us about the actual structure of perception, but we know in fact that a Greek like Aristotle, who knew nothing of neural impulses or about retinal rods and cones, was capable of speaking very meaningfully about vision and the structure of visual experience (pp. 42, 47). This is because the structures of experience are logically independent of and "transcendentally" prior to their physiological conditions.

THE OBJECT-OF-THOUGHT AND THE ORDERS OF REALITY

James's discussion of the "Orders of Reality" is one of the aspects of the *Principles* which has already received a considerable amount of discussion on the part of phenomenologists, particularly by Alfred Schutz and Aron Gurwitsch.[46] The more recent commentaries of Wild and Wilshire link this discussion to James's radical empiricism.[47] Wilshire writes:

> I think that all the talk through the decades of James's "pluralism" has tended to obscure the demise of dualism in the *Principles* and the emergence of phenomenal monism and incipient phenomenology. The talk

arose from viewing James in only one limited historical context: his attack on the peculiar monism of the absolute idealists. It is an example of being confined to the closet of contemporaneity. (p. 58)

Wild argues that there is no incompatibility between James's "pluralism" and his "radical empiricism" since for him empiricism is "the ultimate philosophy" (p. 209). James's "pluralism" in any case comes down to no more than the conviction that the true philosopher must avoid substituting theory and speculation for the variegated diversity of experience, must never cut himself off from all vicissitudes and sinuosities of the real. When James rejected monism it was because he saw in it a sterile "metaphysical" attempt to reduce the wealth and variety of experience to a few empty principles which would save us from further work and dispense us from the contingencies of the future revision of our theories.

> While I talk and the flies buzz, a sea-gull catches a fish at the mouth of the Amazon, a tree falls in the Adirondack wilderness, a man sneezes in Germany, a horse dies in Tartary, and twins are born in France. What does that mean? Does the contemporaneity of these events with one another and a million others as disjointed, form a rational bond between them, and unite them into anything that means for us a world?[48]

"The world" is not an achieved totality but a continually enlarging horizon in which novelties without number await us. It is, says James, a "multiversum" rather than a universum,[49] a pluralistic and kaleidoscopic convergence of viewpoints, all of which are partial and any one of which carries only a presumptive validity, which will not permit themselves to be reduced to any all-inclusive system before the whole of experience has taken place, which is to say never.

But, on a more fundamental level, there is in James's radical empiricism what we might call a methodological "monism of the phenomenon" (to take a phrase from Sartre)[50] which necessarily results from his discovery that thoughts (as "acts") and things referred to by thoughts can be identified and specified only through the "object of thought."[51] The "object of thought," according to James, belongs neither to the physical world (the "topic," or reference of thought) nor to the stream of experience but is rather the means by which we can objectify both consciousness, on the one hand, and things in the world, on the other. The "object of thought" (which in chapter twelve of the *Principles* he designates by the term "conception") is the "function" through which the mind intends "a permanent subject of discourse."

It properly denotes neither the mental state nor what the mental state signifies, but the relation between the two, namely, the *function of* the mental state in signifying just that particular thing. (I, 461)

This is very close to the properly phenomenological notion of the *phenomenon,* and that this is so is borne out by James's discussion of the "orders of reality." At the outset James adopts a distinction found in Brentano, and one which is pivotal for Husserl's phenomenology, between the mere presentation of an object to consciousness and my "belief in" or "assent to" what is presented in this cognitive experience. It would not be amiss to suggest that James's discussion of the various ways in which objects presented to consciousness become objects of "belief" is one of the sources of Husserl's own distinctions between the various doxic modalities which affect experienced objects. For phenomenology, the notion of "object" (or phenomenon: that which appears *just as* it appears) is a more fundamental notion than the notions of "being" or "thing" or "reality" because modes of being are correlated to modes of experiencing. The world of experience comprises many different categories of objects (Husserl's "regional ontologies") and James begins by listing a plethora: there are perceptual objects, past objects, remembered objects, imaginary and unreal objects, hallucinatory objects, fictional objects, formal or categorial objects, number systems, scientific laws, theoretical objects, scientific and religious entities, "idols of the tribe," particular myths, etc., all of which are given as belonging to different but internally coherent *systems* which constitute the "orders of reality" or the "many worlds" of experience (II, 287ff., 291ff.).[52]

An object of consciousness—just *as* object—is believed in and assented to as "real" as long as, and to the extent that, it fits into a context or system of congruent objects "which nothing contradicts" and which "tolerate" or are compatible with it.

> *The first sensation which an infant gets is for him the universe.* And the universe which he later comes to know is nothing but an amplification and an implication of that first simple germ. . . . In his dumb awakening to the consciousness of *something there,* a mere *this* . . . the infant encounters an object in which (though it be given in a pure sensation) all the "categories of the understanding" are contained. It has objectivity, unity, substantiality, causality, in the full sense in which any later object or system of objects has these things. Here the young knower meets and greets his world. (II, 8)

One achieves a sense of "unreality" or disbelief in the "real" existence of something only when it is experienced as incompatible with something else in our world; while we are dreaming, our dreams are the whole of reality for us; it is only after we awake and can compare these experiences to those of another order that we are able to distinguish the world of dreaming from the world of perceptual reality. "Any object," writes James, "which remains uncontradicted is *ipso facto* believed and posited as absolute reality" (II, 289). Take the famous example which James borrows from Spinoza, of thinking of a "winged horse."

> That horse, its wings, and its place, are all equally real. That horse exists no otherwise than as winged, and is moreover really there, for that place exists no otherwise than as the place of that horse, and claims as yet no connection with the other places of the world. But if with this horse I make an inroad into the *world otherwise known*, and say, for example, "That is my old mare Maggie, having grown a pair of wings where she stands in her stall," the whole case is altered; for now the horse and place are identified with a horse and place otherwise known, and *what* is known of the latter objects is incompatible with what is perceived with the former. "Maggie in her stall with wings! Never!" The wings are unreal, then, visionary. I have dreamed a lie about Maggie in her stall. (II, 289)

What is important here is that there can be consciousness of various consistent worlds of mythology or of imagination in which such "unreal" objects of consciousness as winged horses fit perfectly well, about which true and false statements can be made, in which certain things can happen and others not, which have their own specific temporal, spatial, and other qualities. The world of perception is not the world of scientific explanation, and the world of science is not the world of religion or art. We effortlessly live in several worlds at once and move from one to the other without confusing them—at least for long. We discover and live in the categorial systems of mathematics and logic as objectively and coercively as we live in the world of perception without ever taking numbers for perceptual objects, and it is one of the tasks of phenomenology to distinguish and then interrelate the structures of perceptual consciousness with those of imagination, memory, categorial thought, scientific and religious constructs, etc. Of the objects of all these activities of consciousness we can say that, as objects, they are all "real" in their proper sense. "Every object we think of gets at last referred to one world or another of this or of some similar list," James writes. "Each world *whilst it is attended to* is real after its own fashion; only the reality lapses with the attention" (II, 293).

Degrees and kinds of belief (*doxa*) are therefore correlated with the various systems or "regions" of objects which consciousness distinguishes and in which it dwells. But there is an *order* among these various worlds and, at the limit, they are found to be all aspects and possibilities of the unified lifeworld which is the ultimate horizon of all experience. James does more than provide a preliminary map of the various orders of reality. He goes on to suggest that there is one sense of the word "real" which is paramount and which provides us with the primary analogue in terms of which the various orders of reality can be unified. In so doing he anticipates Husserl and Merleau-Ponty in locating the primary sense of reality in perceptual consciousness.[53] Analysis discovers not only that there are various orders of reality, with their distinctive and distinguishing qualities and structures, but that all these various orders are correlated to one and the same consciousness, a consciousness which can perceive, remember, imagine, and think the *same world* by adopting various poetic attitudes towards it. There is for consciousness the possibility of entertaining the *same object* in more than one way. This consciousness is, however, always situated in a perceptual place which is, for it, the inescapable corporeally embodied center of its world. The lived-time and lived-space of this perceptual existence, perspectivally situated within a world of other factually given physical bodies, other persons, and to some extent determined by its "practical interests," has the peculiar quality of always being marginally and subliminally present even when we are lost in other worlds of thought or imagination, whereas the converse is not the case. This perceptual embodiment gives us our primary sense of reality on which all others are founded. It is impossible here to go further into James's contributions to what has come to be called, after Merleau-Ponty, the thesis of the "primacy of perception" in the various orders of experience;[54] we can best illustrate it, in any case, by examining James's conception of the self.

JAMES'S NON-EGOLOGICAL THEORY OF CONSCIOUSNESS

Sartre, Gurwitsch, and the early Husserl (of *Logische Untersuchungen*) all defend a non-egological theory of consciousness. Since we find in James's thought the same motives which inspired these later phenomenological reflections, it will be of interest to examine briefly his own position. It is here, also, that we will be able to understand why both Wild and Wilshire conclude that James's thought leads in the direction of *existential* (as opposed to "pure" transcendental) phenomenology.[55]

James's development of his theory of the self in its relationship to consciousness is one of the most "dramatic" elements in his *Principles*.[56] It is strewn across several chapters of the *Principles* and concluded in the *Essays on Radical Empiricism*, with the result that the manner in which he first set up the problem is, in the end, completely negated. In chapter nine of the *Principles*, on the stream of consciousness, he had begun in his usual "dualistic" fashion by saying that every thought is "owned," is personal, and "mine" (I, 226). No mind can think or experience for another. "Absolute insulation, irreducible pluralism," he writes, "is the law." The primary datum is, therefore, in some sense egological and "solipsistic." If two minds think of the constellation of stars, Orion, there are *two* thoughts and *one* constellation; the "being" of a thought is distinct from its cognitive function.

> But, writes Wilshire, the upshot of Chapter Ten is that the self is not a sealed container full of intrinsically private thoughts. It is as if the self were blasted open and distributed across the face of the lived-world. The result: I can know that I think of Orion only after I know what Orion is, i.e., something anybody else with eyes can see too. There is total reversal: the problem is not how thoughts can be public but how they can be private.[57]

What James achieves by his gradual analysis is a distinction between the "self" and "consciousness," and the manner in which he does this is not essentially different from that adopted by Sartre though the two theories were developed utterly independently of one another.[58] To common sense it seems obvious that I can, through reflection, divide the whole of reality into "me" and "not-me," and in a sense this is true. But *what* we discover by reflection (or "introspection") in our attempt to grasp the very *being* of consciousness is not consciousness itself but just another "object" of consciousness—which in this case is "myself." This "self" is the most "interesting," the most highly prized and valued ("warm"), the most intimate and always present object in my field of awareness, but it is not consciousness itself. It is "out there" with other objects—only not so far out as the others. Consciousness is the stream of "thoughts themselves," says James, and he finds that he cannot "turn around quickly enough" to catch them. When consciousness tries to come to itself and reflect upon itself, it discovers an objective self which appears to it as its owner and the causal source of its acts.[59]

James's phenomenological description of the sense of the self is quite elaborate and contains many insights of great value which, if justice were to be done them, would have to be laid out in much greater detail than we can permit ourselves here. His most important conclusion is that the self, upon reflection, appears not to be a stable, isolable, self-identical thing at all, but a "fluctuating material"; my "self" is not something fixed but rather something that appears differently in different contexts and from diverse perspectives. There is the "material self" ("we feel the whole cubic mass of our body all the while" [I, 333]), but my "self" is not experienced purely and simply as something which exists only within the physical contours of my body; it greatly transcends such physical limits; it is in some sense "the sum total" of all I can call "mine" (I, 291): the works of my hands, my ideas, my opinions and convictions, my active life and my profession, my family and children, those I care for, their personal histories and involvements, etc. If someone attacks what is "mine," he attacks *me*, and an attack on my collection of paintings, my reputation, my friends, my philosophical convictions, may be regarded as far more serious than a physical assault on my body. "Properly speaking," writes James, "a man has as many social selves as there are individuals who recognize him and carry an image of him in their mind. To wound any one of these his images is to wound him" (I, 294).[60] There is, finally, a man's "inner subjective being," his experience of being an active and emotional source of experience (a "spiritual self").

Here we again meet the paradox of the intentionality of consciousness. When we turn to consciousness, to examine it in its own specific being, we find not an "entity" distinct from its objects but just this cognitive *function* of having objects. If I, then, examine all the objects— distinct from all the others in my field of awareness—which I can call "mine" or "me," I find that their unity consists in their all being *related* (in various complex ways) to my experience of being embodied in a place. If I distinguish the "empirical" or "objective" self, the *me* as it is diversely experienced, from the ego conceived as an active and emotional source, and attempt to thematize just the "being denoted by the pronoun I" (I, 298)—*the central active* self—what do I discover?

> *Whenever my introspective glance succeeds in turning round quickly enough to catch one of these manifestations of spontaneity in the act, all it can ever feel distinctly is some bodily process, for the most part taking*

place within the head . . . the acts of attending, assenting, negating, making an effort, are felt as movements of something in the head . . . I cannot think in visual terms . . . without feeling a fluctuating play of pressures, convergences, divergences, and accommodations in my eyeballs. . . . In consenting and negating . . . the opening and closing of the glottis play a great role . . . and, less distinctly, the movements of the soft palate. . . . My glottis is like a sensitive valve, intercepting my breath instantaneously at every mental hesitation or felt aversion. . . . The feeling of the movement of this air is . . . one strong ingredient of the feeling of assent. . . . In a sense, then, it may be truly said that . . . *the "Self of selves," when carefully examined, is found to consist mainly of the collection of these peculiar motions in the head or between the head and the throat*. (I, 300–301)

This discovery, as Wilshire notes (p. 129), seems to shock James himself, and leads him to ask his famous question: *Does Consciousness Exist?*[61] If "the innermost sanctuary" of the self is found to be only the experience of embodiment, then it must follow that *all* that is experienced is strictly speaking "objective."

This Objective falls asunder . . . as "Self" . . . [and] "not-Self"; and . . . over and above these parts there *is* nothing save the fact that they are known, the fact of the stream of thought being there as the indispensable subjective condition of their being experienced at all. (I, 304)

Objectively, the self is "a collection of cephalic movements of 'adjustments' which, for want of attention and reflection, usually fail to be perceived and classed as what they are" (I, 305). Over and above this, there is not "something more" in the sense that there emerges another "entity," an innermost *I* or transcendental *Ego*. There is only the "stream of *Scious*ness pure and simple, thinking objects . . . some of which . . . it calls a 'Me' " (I, 304).

James is not here taking a materialistic position; he could say something like Sartre: "Without being a materialist, I have never distinguished the soul from the body."[62] Consciousness is not given in experience as something independent of the body, except as the cognitive function which, over and above *being* itself, *knows* itself. What it *knows* and what it takes itself to be is, moreover, not just this physical body, this little piece of *res extensa*, but a *self* which exhibits feelings, moods, interests, states of mind, dispositions, which takes on roles, holds positions, and develops into a distinctive and unique force in the world of men. When consciousness turns towards itself, it is this objective "self" in which it is interested, by which it is fascinated, etc. My self is not first and foremost my "mere principle of conscious identity," "my pronoun I," "my pure Ego," but all the things which "arouse feeling and connote emotional worth," all my "phenomenal and perishable powers," "my loves and hates," "willingnesses and sensibilities," etc. (I, 320–23). The various "selves" which I cognize at different times, the ones with which I identify myself and whose side I take, are not all reducible to my material position or physical drives, but they all have this in common that all these selves carry as a part of their meaning a reference to my body.

> Unless his consciousness were something more than cognitive, unless it experienced a partiality for certain of the objects, which, in succession, occupy its ken, it could not long maintain itself in existence; for, by an inscrutable necessity, each human mind's appearance on this earth is conditioned upon the integrity of the body with which it belongs, upon the treatment which that body gets from others, and upon the spiritual dispositions which use it as their tool, and lead it either towards longevity or destruction. *Its own body, then, first of all, its friends next, and finally its spiritual dispositions, must be the supremely interesting OBJECTS for each human mind.* (I, 323)

Let us focus briefly on two of the principal results of James's analysis (without claiming that these in any way exhaust the implications of his investigation). (1) It is, first of all, correctly noted by all three of the commentators whose work we have mentioned[63] that, in this discovery (that the lived body is given as an "object" which is at least concomitantly experienced with every other object of experience, and is that object in terms of which other objects are themselves located and objectified with respect to one another and with respect to the "self" (or "selves") of the experiencing subject) James is touching upon one of the major theses developed by such existential phenomenologists as Sartre and Merleau-Ponty, i.e., the body itself is at the core of experience and the origin of reality—"the *fons et origo* of all reality" he says in another place (II, 296). James did more than merely state this thesis. He employs it to solve the "empiricist" and "associationist" problem of self-identity. In the *Principles* he writes:

> . . . the body, and central adjustments, which accompany the act of thinking, in the head. *These are the real nucleus of our personal identity,* and it is their actual existence, realized as a solid fact, which make us say "as sure *as I exist,* those past facts were part of myself." (I, 341)

The self is found to be the "same" through a series of experiences in the same way in which any other *object* of consciousness can always again be experienced as the "same" as was meant in an earlier experience, but the body, as experienced, has a special constitutive role in the experience of sameness, and therefore in all cognition.

> The world experienced (otherwise called the "field of consciousness") comes at all times with our body as its centre, centre of vision, centre of action, centre of interest. Where the body is is "here"; all other things are "there" and "then" and "that." These words of emphasized position imply a systematization of things with reference to a focus of action and interest which lies in the body; and the systematization is now so instinctive (was it ever not so?) that no developed or active experience exists for us at all except in that ordered form. So far as "thoughts" and "feelings" can be active, their activity terminates in the activity of the body, and only through first arousing its activities can they begin to change those of the rest of the world. The body is the storm centre, the origin of co-ordinates, the constant place of stress in all that experience-train. Everything circles around it and is felt from its point of view. The "I" then, is primarily a noun of position, just like "this" and "here."[64]

It is our experience of our own bodies which "gives us an unceasing sense of personal existence" (I, 333) and, in some sense, the problem of self-identity as well as the problem of objectification in general can be solved only by elaborating a concept of the body-subject, one of whose "functions," only obliquely experienced, is to cognize the world and itself.

(2) But here we come to the second and even more important result of James's analysis: Since consciousness is wholly world-directed, outside of itself even in cognizing itself, its acts and states cannot be examined except in terms of their "objects," by making a detour through the experienced life-world. Consciousness discovers itself situated among bodies and recognizes its own body as its "self." But what, then, is *consciousness?* It cannot *be* its "self" because it is "the indispensable subjective condition" (I, 304) of the experience of the "self" and all other objects given with and coordinated to the self.

It is difficult to speak of consciousness ("the pure activity of our thought taking place as such" (I, 333) because consciousness is a "function" or condition of all objectification and is thus necessarily pre-objective.

> This *condition* of the experience is not one of the *things experienced* at the moment; this knowing is not immediately *known*. It is only known in subsequent reflection. (I, 304)

Since consciousness, in its activity of cognizing or objectification is always *actual* and *present*, it can never grasp itself as an "object"—"It may feel its own immediate existence . . . but nothing can be known *about* it until it be dead and gone" (I, 341). Consciousness can take its just completed past acts as objects of reflection, but even as it does so "the present moment of consciousness" must always remain "the darkest in the whole series," because the act of consciousness which takes itself as an object must always necessarily escape objectification—as the "indispensable subjective condition" of such objectification.

It therefore seems perfectly justifiable to say that James adopted a non-egological theory of consciousness on phenomenological grounds. He rejects the theory of the "substantial soul" because the soul, as a principle of explanation, cannot be experienced. He recognizes the "logical respectability" of such a doctrine but "hardens his heart" against it because it is an unnecessary hypothesis to account for the experienced continuousness of the stream of consciousness. He considers Kant's theory of the transcendental Ego to be "as ineffectual and windy an abortion as Philosophy can show" (I, 365),[65] and the reason he thinks this is the same which Sartre gives for rejecting what he takes to be Husserl's later egological theory of consciousness.

> Consciousness [James writes] . . . can be fully described without supposing any other agent than a succession of perishing thoughts, endowed with the functions of appropriation and rejection, and of which some can know and appropriate or reject objects already known, appropriated, or rejected by the rest. (I, 342)[66]

Consciousness, according to James, is thus not another entity juxtaposed to the entities it knows, with an internal structure of its own, but is rather the "function" of objectification; its forms and structure come from its objects. It can, of course, take its just completed acts as objects, and thus cognize itself as being the same through time, by identifying and "appropriating" its just completed acts as its own. But what it grasps in such a reflexive activity is not the present objectifying function, which always eludes its grasp by one step, but rather its "objective" being as an embodied "self."[67] Consciousness as the "indispensable subjective condition" of such objectification can never be fully thematized or brought to the level of full reflection; it is, in the language of later phenomenologists, a "pre-reflexive" or "pre-thematic" awareness *that*—which is the experienced condition of all reflexive awareness of *what*.[68]

NOETIC FREEDOM

"An idea," James wrote, "neither is what it knows, nor knows what it is" (I, 477). It is clear from the context that "idea" here means the process of "thought" or "feeling"—terms James uses to designate any given "pulse" in the stream of consciousness. Taken in this context, James's theory of consciousness is, as we have begun to see, quite similar to Sartre's: "Consciousness is consciousness *of* something. This means that . . . consciousness is born oriented towards a being which is not itself. . . . To say that consciousness is consciousness of something means that . . . [it] must be what it is not and not be what it is."[69]

Though we cannot do so here, it would be possible to show that Sartre and James build their ethical theories on this similar epistemological foundation: that consciousness experiences itself as being radically independent of its "objects" (and all "things") and that this experience of noetic distance, this experience of *not* being inserted in the causal structure of the determinate and determined things which it "knows," provides the basic phenomenological (i.e., experiential) foundation of moral as well as "noetic" freedom.

The most important contribution of Wild's study of James, in my opinion, lies in his discussion of James's ethics and, in particular, his conception of "noetic" freedom as the basic concept of James's ethical theory (pp. 127, 201, 260ff., 273ff., 314). This enables Wild to correct Ralph Barton Perry's widely repeated interpretation (that James's ethics is "a version of utilitarianism based on the principle of inclusiveness"); neither Dewey nor Perry were at all sensitive to James's notion of the experience of the free act and, when they read all he was writing about it, they tended simply to cancel it out in their own minds as just another sign of "his neurasthenia" which would best be passed over in silence (pp. 274ff.).

What traditional ethicists have wanted to know of James, as of every other philosopher, was how his theory could be classified, how he would define the good: Is it the actualization of a potency? Is it intelligibility, satisfaction of basic needs, the avoidance of suffering, social usefulness, self-realization, etc.? But the fact of the matter is that James considered the elaboration of an ethical theory which would fit into such categories or sub-divisions of similar universal principles slightly fatuous.

> Think of Zeno, and Epicurus, think of Calvin and Paley, think of Kant and Schopenhauer, of Herbert Spencer and John Henry Newman, no longer as one-sided champions of special ideals, but as school-masters deciding what all must think—and what more grotesque topic could a satirist wish for on which to exercise his pen? The fabled attempt of Mrs. Partington to arrest the rising tide of the North Atlantic with her broom was a reasonable spectacle compared with their effort to substitute the content of their clean-shaven systems for that exuberant mass of goods with which all human nature is in travail, and groaning to bring to the light of day.[70]

Though Wild does not make the comparison with Sartre which we have suggested, his own account of James's ethical thought suggests even more numerous parallels (which we cannot pursue here); of Sartre as of other existentialists it has been said that his ethics is everywhere and nowhere in his philosophy. There is no specific chapter on "ethics" in the table of contents of any of his books; he does not recognize it as a separate branch of philosophy, and yet it pervades everything he writes. The same can be said of James: "One might say that James's whole philosophy is an ethics," Wild writes (p. 265). If one had to categorize James, the closest one could get would be to call him a "noetic voluntarist."[71] He is a "voluntarist" because he recognizes no criterion of choice independent of the free act itself; but he is a "noetic" voluntarist because, for him, will is a function of attention and attention is a function of cognition. James does not separate knowing and willing; to attend to something—which, in itself, is an act of knowing—is—in so far as one could be attending to something else— an act of volition. And, as we have seen above, James discusses belief in terms of volition also: "Belief resembles more than anything what in the psychology of volition we know as consent" (II, 283).

There is, in James, no univocal definition of the good, nor is there any refutation of determinism other than the decision: "My first act of free will shall be to believe in free will."[72] His philosophy of the free act is wholly bounded by the world of experience; it is founded on *an experience* which can be analyzed and perhaps "explained away" by determinists in many different ways, all of which are nevertheless equally irrelevant because within this world in which I live my life, practice my profession, collaborate with my friends, and thwart my enemies I cannot but experience myself to be free. That is, in the phenomenal order, an ultimate fact which determinisms can circumscribe theoretically but not eliminate practically.

The first definition of freedom which James accepted (from Renouvier), namely, "the sustaining of a thought *because* I choose to when I might have other thoughts,"[73] contains in germ the whole of his later theory. Later on, when he speaks of the "choice" one makes of his world, he connects it with the entertaining of various possible thoughts about the same topic.

> The whole distinction of real and unreal, the whole psychology of belief, disbelief, and doubt, is thus grounded on two mental facts—first, that we are liable to think differently of the same; and second, that when we have done so, we can choose which way of thinking to adhere to and which to disregard. (II, 290)

Slightly later he connects this to the nature of attention:

> Each thinker . . . has dominant habits of attention; and these *practically elect from among the various worlds some one to be for him the world of ultimate realities*. From this world's objects he does not appeal. Whatever contradicts them must get into another world or die. (II, 293–94)

It is unimportant that various men have more or less fixed habits of attention, or that some objective situations virtually impose themselves on our attention and cannot be ignored. What is important is that we interpret and give meaning to the stimuli, that we notice certain configurations and ignore others equally interesting from a different point of view, that we are always more interested in one part of an object than another, in one possibility than another, and that this selectivity on the part of attention is already a choosing.

> The mind selects again. It chooses certain of the sensations to represent the thing most *truly*, and considers the rest as its appearances, modified by the conditions of the moment. Thus my tabletop is named *square*, after but one of an infinite number of retinal sensations which it yields, the rest of them being sensations of two acute and two obtuse angles; but I call the latter *perspective* views, and the four right angles the *true* form of the table, and erect the attribute squareness into the table's essence, for aesthetic reasons of my own. (I, 285)

Reasoning itself depends on the ability of the mind "to break up the totality of the phenomenon" into parts and then "to pick out from among these the particular one which, in our given emergency, may lead to the proper conclusion" (I, 287). This ability of the mind to "attend to" what is presented to it, to select, to emphasize, to organize, in short to see the possible in the actual is "the very root of judgment, character and will" (I, 424); it is what distinguishes consciousness from its objects and makes a man *compos sui,* aware and responsible. The study of "free choice" is therefore a much wider topic for James than the traditional question about the freedom of the will conceived as a special faculty; it pervades the whole of his thought, and since choosing, believing, and acting are the very source of evaluative activity, his ethical thought pervades his entire work. When he does come to the "psychology of volition" proper, he makes his "noetic" view of freedom fully explicit: "The essential achievement of the will, in short, when it is most 'voluntary', is to *attend to* a difficult object, and hold it fast before the mind" (II, 561). There *is* a "drama" of freedom and responsibility, and there is a problem of training the will, but "the whole drama is a mental drama. The whole difficulty is a mental difficulty, a difficulty with an object of our thought" (II, 564). To bridge the chasm between possibility and actuality, to make what "could be" become real, is, for James, the ethical problem *par excellence;* he is a pragmatist and a meliorist because he believes in "belief" and "action" brought about on the basis of consciousness' distinctness from its "objects of thought." For consciousness *everything could be* other than it is. We are, at least, to some extent, the masters of our meanings (II, 655), and, to this extent, the world will not be completed without us.

CONCLUSION

The second major contribution of Wild's book lies in its attempt to take into consideration James's later writings on pragmatism, on religious experience, and on other topics in order to arrive at a more coherent and systematic view of James's thought than has yet been achieved. But this part of his work (the last five chapters) is to a large extent still programmatic, and he is content to point the way forward. I think that, on the basis of his work, a number of fruitful suggestions for future phenomenological investigations can be made. One of the most interesting of these would be a phenomenological assessment of James's pragmatism, both as it develops internally from the lines already laid down in the *Principles,* and in relation to the "pragmatism" we find in Husserl, Merleau-Ponty, and other phenomenologists. Such an investigation would not be limited to the pragmatic theory of truth; both Husserl and Merleau-Ponty develop the notion of consciousness which, in the most fundamental sense, is more of an "I can do" than a contemplative receptor or copier of reality.[74] Moreover, the notion of "the retroactivity of truth" which Merleau-Ponty develops in his ethical writings[75] seems to be but an independent formulation of insights which James enunciated as early as "The Sentiment of Rationality" and then orchestrated in his pragmatist period. The study of this question would also lead to a clearer and more accurate assessment of the relationship of moral and pragmatic "truth" to truth in the categorial sense, to a deeper study of how perceptual consciousness and categorial consciousness are related—a problem central both to phenomenology and to James but one which is quite neglected in the present literatuare.

Wild deals more fully with James's contributions to the phenomenology of religious experience.[76] Better than most commentators on James, he develops James's interest in the phenomena of courage, struggle, bold and strenuous action, risk, heroism, the "serious" situations, the "strenuous" life (pp. 291ff.). Wild also shows a fine sensitivity to the relative moral and intellectual qualities of the "morbid-minded" as opposed to the "healthy-minded" in James's writings on religion (pp. 301ff.), and he convincingly describes some of the boundaries which divide "the religious" from "the ethical" (p. 316) though, here too, a good deal remains yet to be said. In his attitude towards religious experience James adopted a phenomenological or descriptive approach—an effort to get at the essential meaning of certain phenomena such as prayer, sanctity, mystical exaltation, and so on, without ever "psychologizing" them or reducing them to their physiological infrastructures. Unlike almost all other philosophers of religion, he avoids giving a univocal definition of what it is. His method is to take a number of paradigm cases, to "arrange them in their series," and thus delineate some essential structures of the experience under investigation. On the whole Wild's discussion, excellent as it is, is far from comprehensive and is oriented more toward the conclusions in the realm of the philosophy of religion, toward which James was groping, than toward his method just as such, or what can be gained from its further development. It seems to me, therefore, that his account will but whet the appetite of his phenomenologically inclined readers and that one major importance of his book lies in the future work it will stimulate.

Two conclusions, in particular, will fly in the face of the readers of these books. (1) While he has in the past appeared to some to be little more than "a brilliant and slightly irresponsible amateur"[77] in philosophy, James emerges more and more as one of the pivotal philosophers of the contemporary world. "In spite of the racy surface of his style," Wilshire writes, "he is often an obscure and headcracking writer. It is not hard to understand why he had such strong appeal for major thinkers like Husserl, Dewey, Bergson, and the later Wittgenstein, and why he is so often cavalierly dismissed by thinkers of lesser rank" (p. 180).

(2) Connected with this pivotal historical importance are the truly astounding number of paths he opened up, the number of theories he fathered, the number of subjects he took up and advanced. There is hardly any philosophical topic or problem which fell under his attention to which he did not make some original contribution. This very dispersion of his interests, in psychology, in the theory of knowledge and theory of the emotions, in ethics and religion, in pragmatism, meliorism, radical empiricism, and pluralism, not to mention his political and educational activities and his contributions to psychical and parapsychological research, has led many commentators on his thought to overemphasize its unsystematic and occasional character. But in the light of the recently begun phenomenological evaluation of his writings, there has come the realization that, fully explicit or not, there is a much greater unity of method and coherence of doctrine among his various theories and -isms than has been hitherto recognized. This is not to say that we are now going to reduce James's thought to a neat system; to this his ideas will always remain recalcitrant. More than any other philosopher, with the possible exception of Husserl, James felt that he was a "beginner." One month before his death, on July 26, 1910, he gave a written instruction that his last work should bear the subtitle: "A Beginning of an Introduction to Philosophy." In the face of "Philosophy," the philosopher is always a novice and a beginner, and, again like Husserl, James was distrustful of finished, systematic treatises or achieved systems of thought which needed no further revision. He did not believe that any man could see well enough or far enough into the world of the manifold to bring it all under some one universal thought or reason. But, on the other hand, though he confessed that he did not possess "science," he most clearly did possess "the hope of a science," and his own contributions were, in the end, perhaps more consistent and systematic than he knew.

> It is not that we are all nature but some point which is reason, but that all is nature and all is reason too. We shall see, damn it, we shall see. . . .[78]

III William James's Phenomenology of Religious Experience

The aim of this study is to investigate William James's contributions to the phenomenology of religious experience. To some it may appear strange that James "the pragmatist" should so forthrightly and without apologies be incorporated into the phenomenological viewpoint.[1] But I want to show that James's methodological contributions to the study of religious experience are not only more sound phenomenologically than some of the studies which have, under the influence of Husserl, up to now explicitly invoked the phenomenological method, but that they are also the first to establish any solid basis for a true phenomenology of religious experience.

Religious Phenomena

Husserl, himself, was not—at least throughout most of his life— much interested in religious phenomena.[2] His major successors, Heidegger, Sartre, and Merleau-Ponty, have likewise taken phenomenology to be a philosophy of the *Diesseitigkeit*, and have thus almost completely neglected religious experience. Heidegger has said that in the present state of philosophical thought it is impossible to pose questions about religious experience.[3] While it is true that Sartre is obsessed with the idea of God, both as it acts in human experience,[4] and as the self-contradictory "limit concept" in terms of which we must understand the eternally futile attempt of consciousness to give itself "substance" or "being," he has certainly not given any sympathetic at-

49

tention to the phenomena of religious experience as such. Merleau-Ponty alone among the major disciples of Husserl has mentioned the intrinsic interest and value of such an investigation from the phenomenological point of view, and he left a place for such a branch of phenomenology in his own program.[5] However, like Husserl, he did little more than express an interest in the possibility of such an investigation and made no contribution of his own toward fulfilling it. Even Gabriel Marcel (to turn to more religious representatives of non-Husserlian phenomenology) has left his original doctoral project, an approach to the phenomenology of mystical experience, incomplete and unpublished. Thus, the founders and "fathers" of the phenomenological movement in Europe have given us nothing in the way of a phenomenology of religious experience.

There is, it is true, a more or less unified school of thought in the history and philosophy of religion, represented by such names as G. Van Der Leeuw, Joachim Wach, Mircea Eliade, Rudolph Otto, and others who have practiced the "phenomenology of religion."[6] The work of this "school," which owes much more to Dilthey than to Husserl, needs no apologist. Basing itself on the late nineteenth-century German *Verstehendepsychologie* and utilizing the classificatory schema inaugurated by Dilthey, this school has developed a comprehensive (*Verstehende*) hermeneutics of religious symbols, institutions, and the like, and has established a more or less universal sociological and anthropological "morphology" (Eliade) or "typology" (Wach) for the interpretation of historical religions. The concrete details of such typologies differ from author to author, but they are imbued with a common direction and method. Van Der Leeuw says this method can as well be called "The General Science of Religion," or "Transcendental Psychology," or "Eidology," or even *Formenlehre der religiösen Vorstellungen* as "Phenomenology of Religion," but this last denomination is now the most current and widely accepted.[7]

This last approach to the study of religion is, at least in intention, truly phenomenological. In their various methodological reflections these authors show clearly that they adopt a purely descriptive, phenomenological approach; that such an approach cannot be "normative" or serve as the basis for any theology; finally that it is not pure history or sociology but eidetic inquiry into the essential structures of religious institutions and religious symbols.[8] Van Der Leeuw says that the purpose of such an inquiry is to discover "meanings" or "types" and "structural connections" within and among such "types" which are "neither factual relationships nor causal connections," which are "timeless and need not actually occur in history."[9] And Wach writes: "Neither history nor psychology can do the job of phenomenology. Neither deduction nor abstraction secures the 'essence' (*eidos*) vouchsafed by the *Wesenschau*."[10] Such a study is clearly not just history, nor is it psychology, textual criticism, metaphysics, or theology.[11] It is a genuine phenomenological attempt to arrive at the ultimate and foundational structures empirically incarnated in the various historical religions. None of these structures is ever exhaustively instantiated in any given historical case. Such a study results in an eidetics (or "typology") of religious expressions (symbols) and institutions common to man as *Homo religiosus*.

Nevertheless, even though none of these authors can be accused of historical relativism or psychologism, their approach to experience is not through direct reflection upon what is immediately given. Instead, it must pass through "the control of philological-archaeological hermeneutics."[12] Van Der Leeuw even seems to identify "phenomenology" in this sense with Dilthey's "hermeneutics." Wach and Eliade also tie their "phenomenology" essentially and necessarily to the history of religions. Thus, rather than being a method (or a "science") in its own right, such phenomenology is the way in which the historian of religions exercises his "understanding" within his own field *qua* historian.[13]

THE PHENOMENOLOGICAL APPROACH

But there is another phenomenological approach possible in this area, and one which would appear to be much closer to what Husserl and Merleau-Ponty envisaged as the properly phenomenological elucidation of this domain of experience. It would be a phenomenology precisely not of *religion*—in some or in all of its manifestations—but of *religious experience as such*. It would be a study not of historical and philological origins of religious meanings and symbols, but of the foundations of such meanings in consciousness itself. The *Ursprung* of such meanings would not be found through historical, sociological, and anthropological investigations but through an analysis of actual, present religious experience. It would be, in short, less a hermeneutics of texts and institutions than a turn to naive, unreflective experience, as we find it prior to any theory or doctrine about it.

This is the orientation of William James in his *Varieties of Religious Experience,* and this is what radically distinguishes him from other phenomenologists of religion. Though he undertook these investigations utterly independently of and without any reference to Husserl, the approach he takes would seem to be more directly Husserlian than that of the "school" which formally claims the name. I am not, of course, claiming that these two approaches are mutually incompatible or irreconcilable; they clearly are not. I am, rather, claiming that William James was the *first* to attempt a phenomenology of religious experience in an experiential sense, and I would point out that he has had almost no successor in this endeavor up to the present time. As is characteristic of James's contributions to philosophy, he but opened up a way which he left incomplete and unfinished at his death, a method which has been unaccountably neglected by his successors and disciples; and I would suggest that by prosecuting this method we would discover another of the remarkable points of convergence between Husserl's philosophy and that of James.[14]

James remarked once, in 1897, that "religion is the great interest of my life,"[15] and when he was offered the Gifford Lectureship in 1898 (it had been suggested already in 1896), he began the systematic collection and analysis of the great mass of material which went into those lectures (1901–2) and which was published as *The Varieties of Religious Experience, a Study in Human Nature* in New York in 1902. This was not a historical study; James had, indeed, very little interest in the social and institutional aspects of religion and considered them rather unimportant.[16] Though he necessarily uses historical documents and the reports of the experiences of others, he does so only in order to understand "what goes on in the single private man," in order to get at the concrete and individual experience itself insofar as possible, and not its "conventional expression." He believed that there were specifically and uniquely religious data or "facts," and he wanted to get at the meaning of these facts. He is very clear, from the outset, that he is not going to present a philosophy of religion but, rather, what we can now rightly call a "phenomenological" description of the whole complex structure of interlocking needs, motives, ideals, desires, feelings, moods, etc., which, taken together, constitute religious experience in its various modalities.

> Religion [he wrote] is the very inner citadel of human life, and the pretension to translate adequately into spread-out conceptual terms a kind of experience in which intellect, feeling and will, all our consciousness and all our subconsciousness together melt in a kind of chemical fusion, would be particularly abhorrent. Let me say then with frankness at the outset, that I believe that no so-called philosophy of religion can possibly

begin to be an adequate translation of what goes on in the single private man, as he livingly expresses himself in religious faith and act.[17]

James *did* hold some elements of a philosophy of religion, at least in the sense of certain conclusions about the nature of consciousness, God, and the universe as a whole, but these are only very sketchily presented in the *Varieties*. James recognizes that they are somewhat gratuitously introduced toward the end of his treatise and does not claim that they are conclusions which strictly or necessarily follow from the descriptive part. He many times expresses his intention to write a sequel to the *Varieties* in which he would expound his religious philosophy in full detail, but he was prevented from undertaking it by his death. In any event James's religious ideas and his positive religious philosophy fall entirely outside the scope of the present investigation. My purpose is not to recapitulate James's conclusions but to study his *method;* not to give an inventory of the results of his work, but to attempt to discern the nature and importance of his methodological contribution.[18] The fact that he himself explicitly distinguishes his purely descriptive approach to the phenomena of religious experience from any metaphysical conclusions or religious philosophy justifies our decision to focus exclusively on his descriptive method.

He states, as the first postulate, that he is not going to investigate, at least for their own sake, questions of the *origins* of religious meanings either historically or psychologically. This would be an interesting approach to religion but it is methodologically distinct from the study of the essential meaning and value of religious experience as it is lived. His approach, he tells us, will not be "dogmatic" (i.e., "rationalistic") but "empiricist." It will not look for conceptual "tests for truth which might dispense us from appealing to the future."[19] Rather than elaborate explanatory hypotheses, he will examine "the immediate content of the religious consciousness" (p. 28). He will adopt "the purely existential point of view" (p. 44) and, "by addressing [himself] directly to the concrete facts" (p. 57), will aim just at "the description of the phenomena" (p. 354).

The first essential distinction to be made is that between the *psychological origin* of certain religious phenomena (such as conversion for instance) and their meaning or "worth." Even should we find evidence of "nervous instability," of "exalted emotional sensibility" in some "religious geniuses" (p. 24), we cannot thereby dismiss them as just so many "hysterics" (p. 205) because, in fact, "the best fruits of religious experience are the best things that history has to show" (p.

207). In other words we cannot either dismiss or exhaustively "explain" the importance and religious genius of Martin Luther because of certain supposed and hypothetical anal-erotic character traits, or account for his doctrine of justification by faith by the fact that he received his inspiration for this interpretation of Paul's Epistle to the Romans while seated on the toilet. James proceeds like Husserl in a methodological attempt to distinguish the "what" (the essence or meaning) of experience from its existential and psychological conditions and origins. Similarly, we could adduce the case of the Russian religious philosopher Vladimir Solovyov, who was subject to religious hallucinations from early in childhood (the periodic visitations of "Holy Wisdom" in feminine form); Solovyov was fully conscious of the hallucinatory character of his experiences but found no reason, in that, to discount their value or to refuse to learn from them.[20]

> Saint Teresa [writes James] might have had the nervous system of the placidest cow, and it would not now save her theology, if the trial of the theology by these other tests should show it to be contemptible. And conversely if her theology can stand these other tests, it will make no difference how hysterical or nervously off her balance Saint Teresa may have been when she was with us here below. (p. 32)

The "medical materialism" which would finish St. Paul by calling his vision on the road to Damascus a "discharging lesion of the occipital cortex," or snuff out St. Francis of Assisi as a "hereditary degenerate," or cancel George Fox's pining for spiritual veracity as a "symptom of a disordered colon" requires that we reduce experience to its psycho-physiological *origins* (p. 29). But experience itself knows nothing of such origins; my life has a meaning and value for me even if I understand nothing of nervous or circulatory systems and even if I have never read a word of psychopathology. The consideration of the various possible causal explanatory hypotheses of behavior is indeed a branch of knowledge but it must be methodologically excised from any consideration of experience as such.

We know from James's philosophy as a whole (his pragmatism, his meliorism, his pluralism) that what chiefly interested him in human behavior ("what makes life significant") were the phenomena of courage, struggle, bold and strenuous action, risk, heroism. He believed that exceptional circumstances generate exceptional inner power and thus he liked to examine the limit cases, when men are under the highest pressure. And this is why the phenomena of religious experience so attracted him, because they give the most illustrative examples of the "strenuous life" (p. 207).

Like the existentialists Sartre, Malraux, Camus, and Dostoevski—and unlike traditional British moralists—James turns to the extreme cases for their illustrative value.[21] This turn is essential to his method. In order to see the varieties of mind which religious experience covers, we must place all these experiences "in their series": "Phenomena are best understood when placed within their series, studied in their germ and in their over-ripe decay, and compared with their exaggerated and degenerated kindred" (p. 294).

To study the ordinary or the conventional "would profit us little." If we are to touch the psychology of religion at all seriously, we must be willing to forget conventionalities, and dive below the smooth and lying official conversational surface" (p. 125). James even called his attempt to get at the "existential study of its conditions" "my pathological programme" (p. 35). " . . . it always leads to a better understanding of a thing's significance to consider its exaggerations and perversions, its equivalents and substitutes and nearest relatives elsewhere" (p. 35).

Thus we can say that James's method is an attempt to arrive at experientially based descriptions of religious phenomena such as conversion, sanctity, mysticism, etc., through an examination of *all* the existential components of such an experience as they are ranged on a continuum from the most ambiguous instances of lowest intensity to the most specific and extreme cases of maximum intensity. It is because the extreme cases allow us to identify the phenomenon most clearly that our knowledge of such cases will enable us to discern the same essential structures more or less partially realized in more amorphous, embryonic, and ambiguous cases. We will, then, come to see that the structures of religious experience discernible in the extreme cases are also present in the most ordinary and banal human behaviors and, indeed, that the religious structures of experience are the most basic and deep-seated of all.

JAMES'S METHOD

William James's greatest single contribution to the study of religious experience was to show us how it could be found, delineated, and defined in a manner which would remain faithful to the uniqueness, the primordiality, and the intrinsic complexity of the experience itself. He did not try to reduce it to one or another of its constituent infrastructures, but to locate all its various levels and aspects as they are in fact interrelated in actual experience.

It is amazing what simple-minded theories philosophers throughout the history of philosophy have propounded to account for religion. Since the time of the early Greeks, philosophers have attempted to give us essential definitions of things. Perhaps because of the very nature of the Greek language, with its system of articles, Socrates and Plato seemed to believe that such things as "Piety," "Courage," "Knowledge," "Justice," and even "the Good," "the Beautiful," "the Useful," etc. could be defined in some one, comprehensive formula, a *to koinon;* and Aristotle established the method for making such definitions through an analysis of species and specific differences. The Greeks of course recognized dimly that there were certain "transcendental" terms which could not be defined in this way; but these were a very restricted number. In recent philosophy, both analytical and existential, we are becoming laboriously more aware of how many of our words and concepts are "polymorphous" and how difficult it is to define anything at all. With his clearly phenomenological approach to this problem, James was well ahead of his time and his lead must now be followed.

Other philosophers have been content to define religious experience by saying that it is *nothing but* so and so. Lucretius identified the essence of the religious impulse with "fear," fear of death, fear of fate, fear of the gods; and, in the full light of the twentieth century, Bertrand Russell finds this view still an acceptable and exhaustive definition of religion.[22] Hume found the source of religion to lie in such natural emotions as terror of death, thirst for revenge, appetite for food, and other biological necessities. Mill identified the source of religion as "hope," and Spencer found it in the experience of "the Unknowable." Schleiermacher defined religion as "the feeling of absolute dependence," and Rudolph Otto said it was "the experience of the holy (*Numen*)." Some have defined it socially, as the need for companionship, in the "brotherhood of men under the fatherhood of God," while others, like the Yogis, have found it to lie exclusively in man's most private, solitary existence *solus cum solo*. Freud perhaps represents the most magnificent and articulated attempt to reduce religious experience to "one thing," to one unique source in human psychology: religion, he said, is a result of sex repression.

It is interesting to note that, though James had read very little Freud and met him only once, near the end of his life (some time after writing the *Varieties*), he was nevertheless aware of the force of this argument and was well aware of the erotogenetic theory of religion and of the large place of sexual symbolism, both normal and abnormal, in religious experience. He cites the coprophilia of Margaret Mary Alacoque, Francis Xavier, St. John of God, and others who cleansed the sores and ulcers of their patients with their tongues (p. 225). The writings of St. Gertrude remind him of "an endless amatory flirtation . . . between the devotee and the deity" (p. 270), and he quotes such passages as the following from Sister Séraphique de la Martinière: "Often the assaults of divine love reduced her almost to the point of death. She used tenderly to complain of this to God. 'I cannot support it,' she used to say. 'Bear gently with my weakness, or I shall expire under the violence of your love' " (pp. 220–21). But, against Freud, he would argue that to reduce religious experience to this one facet of it is a gross over-simplification. "It seems to me that few conceptions are less instructive," he wrote, "than this re-interpretation of religion as perverted sexuality" (p. 27). In fact, he writes, one might just as well interpret religion as a perversion of the respiratory function.

> The Bible is full of the language of respiratory oppression: "Hide not thine ear at my breathing; my groaning is not hid from thee; my heart panteth, my strength faileth me; my bones are hot with my roaring all the night long . . . my soul panteth after thee. . . ." (p. 28)

Religious life depends just as much, he said, on the spleen, the pancreas, and the kidneys as on the sexual apparatus. Human needs for food, warmth, shelter have provided a rich symbolism. While it is true that explicit religious interest in the world develops more or less synchronously with the onset of puberty, so too does every other interest, since it is "the entire higher mental life which awakens during adolescence." As always, James is impatient with any attempt to reduce religious experience to its supposed physiological and psychological origins and, instead, demands that it be taken in its total meaning, as a complex skein of interlocking drives, emotions, desires, motives, ideas, and feelings which must be described in their intentional unity.[23] We must adopt not a monistic but a pluralistic method:

> In the psychologies and in the philosophies of religion, we find the authors attempting to specify just what entity it is. One man allies it to the feeling of dependence; one makes it a derivative from fear; others connect it with the sexual life; others still identify it with the feeling of the infinite; and so on. Such different ways of conceiving it ought themselves

to arouse doubt as to whether it possibly can be one specific thing, . . .
There is religious fear, religious love, religious awe, religious joy, and so
forth. (p. 40)

Religious experiences, we might say, involve the intentionality of
the whole human organism and are specified not by their psychological mechanisms but by their intentional objects.

But religious love is only man's natural emotion of love directed to a religious object; religious fear is only the ordinary fear of commerce, so to
speak, the common quaking of the human breast, in so far as the notion
of divine retribution may arouse it; religious awe is the same organic
thrill which we feel in a forest at twilight, or in a mountain gorge; only
this time it comes over us at the thought of our supernatural relations;
and similarly of all the various sentiments which may be called into play
in the lives of religious persons. As concrete states of mind, made up of a
feeling *plus* a specific sort of object, religious emotions of course are psychic entities distinguishable from other concrete emotions; but there is
no ground for assuming a simple abstract "religious emotion" to exist as a
distinct elementary mental affection by itself, present in every religious
experience without exception. (p. 40)

One could hardly hope for a more explicit statement of the intentional structure of religious experience. In phenomenological research we are concerned with the "meaning" of the experience. Such
meanings are found within the total psychobiological dynamics of individual human life and must be approached as such. It is because of
this primary complexity that "we have really different types of religious experience" (p. 98), and that religious experience does not ex-
hibit any one "essence." If we are to define it, then, we must do so
morphologically. We will not get a clear and distinct concept defined
through genus and specific difference but a polymorphous (James
says "collective") concept, "no one essence, but many characters"
(p. 39).

Religious experience, according to James, then, is a dimension of
human intentional life as a unified whole. It is, we might say, a way in
which a man uses his moods, feelings, emotions, aims, all of which are
given in biological and psychological nature with their own specific
nonreligious teleologies, but which, together and in various mixtures
and gradations, can embody religious intentions and attitudes. Religious experience, then, is an expressive use of the human body. In his

studies on language Merleau-Ponty points out that when a child begins to speak he does so by beginning to use the organs of his body for a purpose which is not "natural" to them. All of the organs which are used in speech (the tongue, lips, palate, throat) have specific biological functions which do not require that they be used for speaking. Language is thus a "superstructure," he says, a phenomenon of a higher order than the biological, but which employs given biological organs for "another purpose," with another intention, "to sing the world."[24] It is somewhat in the same way, I think, that James means us to understand the emergence of religious experience amid the diverse disparate functions of our psychic life. Religious experience does not have any particular bodily organ, is not situated in any specific bodily drive or emotion, but uses them all to express an intention of a higher order.

One of the great difficulties in discussing religious experience, then, lies in the fact that the use of the human psychobiological organism to experience (or "constitute") religious meanings and values is one of the most all-pervasive, most deep-rooted, inescapable, and global of all human behaviors. It can appear in so many guises and so many complex manifestations that the task of laying them all out with exhaustive analytical clarity seems hopeless. There is no man totally devoid of religious feeling in this sense; such feelings are, indeed, "amongst the most important biological functions of mankind" (p. 382). It has even been suggested that the origin of religious experience antedates the appearance of the human race on earth, since some of the higher anthropoids occasionally seem to perform a kind of ritual dance together and deck themselves with leaves and fruit peels as if in an expression of a religious attitude toward the world and one another. Such leaves and fruit peels would then have been the first liturgical vestments. It is not, perhaps, necessary to go so far, but I think James has shown well that religion lies very deep in the structures and substructures of human consciousness. It may be precisely this fact which has prevented philosophers from making much headway up to now in the delineation of religious phenomena.

ARGUMENT BY EXAMPLE: MYSTICAL EXPERIENCE

It is not my intention to recapitulate all the results of James's analyses or repeat all his attempts to give morphological definitions. We must limit ourselves here to one example as an illustration of his method. In modern phenomenological terminology, we could call his

study of "mystical experience" an attempt to establish an eidetic definition of such experience. Nobody, least of all James himself, would
claim that he has discerned all the elements which go to constitute
such an experience, that he has exhaustively grasped the phenomenon and definitively interrelated all its substructures. But he made a
start and gave an example of what such an attempt might achieve.

His analysis of mystical experience is made against the background of certain distinctions already established. He had already distinguished religious experience from its psychological origins. He also
distinguished religious experience from the merely clinical. No doubt
ethical structures are frequently associated with religious experiences, but religion cannot be identified with the ethical; it involves
"impulses to sacrifice" (and self-sacrifice), phenomena of resignation,
and many others which are nonethical in character. Moreover, religion antedates and is independent of purely moral or ethical impulses
and behaviors. Perhaps the distinction of religious from merely ethical phenomena is nowhere better illustrated than in mysticism. Mystical experience is not at all necessary to the ethical life; we can be
"good Christians" or "good Jews" without it. It is something superflu-
ous, above and beyond natural expectations or needs, something
which may require an ethical preparation but which is certainly not
the aim or intention of morality.

Throughout the *Varieties* James reminds us that "my method," as
he terms it, is "empirical" and can thus never bring us to a full vision
of the truth, established once and for all; its conclusions will never be
more than presumptively true and "no empiricist ought to claim ex-
emption from this universal liability" (p. 260). "I may seem to despair
of the very notion of truth. . . . I do indeed disbelieve that we or any
other mortal men can attain on a given day to absolutely incorrigible
and unimprovable truth about such matters of fact as those with which
religions deal" (p. 261).

We know that both temperamentally and philosophically James
had, as he put it, "to fall back on a certain ultimate hardihood, a certain
willingness to live without assurances or guarantees,"[25] and nowhere
are his investigations more precarious than in the field of mysticism.

[Yet] . . . such states of consciousness ought to form the vital chapter
from which the other chapters [of the *Varieties*] get their light. Whether
my treatment of mystical states will shed more light or darkness, I do not
know, for my own constitution shuts me out from their enjoyment almost
entirely. . . . (p. 292)

Thus he proceeds cautiously, and with the limited aim of discovering the "reality" and the "paramount importance" of such ranges of experience. He attempts to range them "in their series" and to establish their general characteristics as they build up from "phenomena which claim no special religious significance" to "those of which the religious pretensions are extreme." The first levels are "sporadic," i.e., they represent "mystical states" which come upon one without special preparation or cultivation, from sudden insights into the deepest significance of common words or situations, to sudden invasions of a sense of mystery and "of the metaphysical duality of things" (i.e., of the transient, phenomenal, unreal character of this world as opposed to a "deeper" level of consciousness and meaning into which we are sometimes plunged in "dreamy states," at times of stress, and other occasions). James discusses the power of nature to produce sudden transports of at least a quasi-mystical character—which he is willing to call "cosmic consciousness"—a sudden grasping of the whole of reality and the realization of one's total identification with it. Such experiences of awe, wonder, or exaltation frequently occur in solitude, when one is walking alone in a forest or along a mountain path, or when gazing at night at the stars. This intuitional grasp of the "oneness" of things is a characteristic note, James believes, of all mystical states from the highest to the lowest, and that is why it is permissible to discover a mystical element in experiences of this kind which almost all men have at some time or other.

Among the lower mystical states James includes the use of alcohol, mescal, chloroform, ether, and other drugs and poisons which are known to bring about temporarily elevated states of consciousness. He writes of them in his inimitable Victorian prose:

The next step into mystical states carries us into a realm that public opinion and ethical philosophy have long since branded as pathological, though private practice and certain lyric strains of poetry seem still to bear witness to its ideality. I refer to the consciousness produced by intoxicants and anaesthetics, especially by alcohol. The sway of alcohol over mankind is unquestionably due to its power to stimulate the mystical faculties of human nature, usually crushed to earth by the cold facts and dry criticisms of the sober hour. Sobriety diminishes, discriminates, and says no; drunkenness expands, unites, and says yes. It is in fact the great exciter of the *Yes* function in man. It brings its votary from the chill periphery of things to the radiant core. It makes him for the moment one with truth. Not through mere perversity do men run after it. To the poor and the unlettered it stands in the place of symphony concerts and of literature; and it is part of the deeper mystery and tragedy of life that whiffs and gleams of something that we immediately recognize as excellent should be vouchsafed to so many of us only in the fleeting earlier phases of what in its totality is so degrading a poisoning. (p. 297)

And, referring to his own experiments with nitrous oxide intoxication, he concludes that our ordinary, waking, "rational" consciousness is but one type of consciousness and that, "parted from it by the filmiest of screens," there are other types and potential forms of consciousness of an entirely different order. This is as far as James is able to go on the basis of his own experience, but he means to show that even those of us who have no access to the higher mystical states are not totally cut off from them or utterly unable to feel what they may mean to those who experience them in a fuller sense. Nearly all men have "such mystical moods" at some time or other, experiences which are their own justification, which need not be proved real to their possessor, which are "ineffable" and cannot be transmitted by talk but which can only be experienced and enjoyed in quietude.

The higher orders of mystical experience are, of course, limited to rather rare individuals and are methodically cultivated as a part of the religious life by certain persons as a means of achieving experimental union with the divine. No major religion has been without mystics in this sense, and James tries to draw together sufficient evidence to delineate certain undeniable characteristics of such experience. First of all, such experiences, though they involve states of feeling, have a decidedly "noetic" quality and give the experiencer an "insight into depths of truth unplumbed by the discursive intellect" (p. 293). Sensorial images play a very large part in such experiences: "They are absolutely sensational in their epistemological quality . . . that is, they are face to face presentations of what seems immediately to exist" (p. 324). On the other hand, the "knowledge" acquired in such states is strictly intuitive and nonconceptualizable. James takes the "consciousness of illumination" to be the most essential mark of mystical states (p. 313), but he notes that this illumination brings with it "no specific intellectual content whatever of its own" (p. 326), that there is no basis in such experience to distinguish the Christian from the Hindu or the Sufi from the Buddhist. When what is experienced is called "God," he is spoken of afterward in negative and often self-contradictory terms: *Deus propter excellentiam non immerito Nihil vocatur* ("God on account of his very excellence is not implausibly called Nothingness") (p. 319).

A final characteristic of mystical experience is that it involves a strong feeling of absorption, unity, and oneness (with God, with the world, with the ocean of consciousness) in which individual identity is lost or at least greatly reduced. This sense of oneness is another universal characteristic of mystical states. Such states seem to come upon the experiencer in attitudes of passivity and cannot be produced or reproduced at will (though certain preparation can be made which would favor their occurrence). Also they are relatively brief and, though never forgotten, cannot be recalled with distinctness. If one were to state, finally, the "pretty distinct theoretic drift" given to such experience by those who have attested to them, they would tend, James believes, to support an "optimistic" and "monistic" religious philosophy.

I will not follow James into his tentative assessment of the value or the "authority" of such experiences for persons who do not have them (he believes them to be "absolutely authoritative" for the experiencer himself) because this would get us beyond the descriptive method which is our sole concern here. I have, by thus recapitulating and paraphrasing one of James's attempts to delineate a given type of religious experience, tried to show how one would establish its "series," so to speak, by the choice of a number of crucial paradigm cases and then describe, insofar as possible, its structure within the total intentionality of the human organism. James has produced no more than the elements of such an eidetic description and it must be extended and complemented in many directions, particularly in the study of those "subliminal," marginal," and other "potential" forms of consciousness which James alludes to but which he is unable to confront directly. He showed, in his own masterly way, what an experiential or phenomenological approach to such religious phenomena might involve.

CONCLUSION

In conclusion, we must pose the final methodological question of the value and limits of phenomenology as a philosophical method in the realm of religious experience. If it is to remain true to its claim to study only and exclusively the structures of experience, it cannot, clearly, answer some kinds of philosophical questions, though it may provide valuable evidence for argument. For example, it cannot come to any theological conclusions or make any statements on the ultimate nature of God, or the ultimate purpose and nature of reality. It can approach God and other noumenal realities only to the extent that they are experienced, and its statements must be restricted to what can be said from such a viewpoint. It is not even certain that phenomenology, in the strictest sense, can use the name of God at all, since the "what" of religious experience (and the "what" of mystical experience) is not always designated in this personal manner by the human experiencer. (It can, of course, speak of the concept of "God" as a cultural institution, etc.)

Thus it might seem that the phenomenology of religious experience, though of the highest value for our study of man—since it deals with perhaps the most foundational and inclusive meaning-structures of human life—is of very limited value to metaphysics and of no value at all to theology. This seems to be James's own view of his work and he does not claim to deduce his own religious philosophy—such as it is—from his descriptions of experience. Yet there may be at least a minimal sense in which something can be said about God: "God is real since he produces real effects" (p. 389). But in another place he wrote: "The divine can mean no single quality, it must mean a group of qualities, by being champions of which in alternations, different men may all find worthy missions." It is quite clear, then, that from this perspective the elaboration of an "objective," "necessary," and "universally true" philosophy of religion is beyond the resources of a pure phenomenology. The question of God can only be posed as the question of the way in which divine and religious power acts in the lives of men, of God not as he is in himself but as he operates in human experience. There seems to be no reason, however, to restrict phenomenological investigations merely to the study of those structures of experience which are common to all men. I see no reason why, after a general phenomenology of religous experience (which was what James had primarily in mind), one could not do more specific phenomenologies of Christian or Jewish or Muslim experience and perhaps, eventually, of even more restricted "worlds" and communities within these common traditions.

That phenomenology is not a "total" philosophy or a "totalitarian" method is clear; there are limits to what such an approach can attain. But at this moment when we have just discovered the unexplored thresholds James opened up for us, we should be more concerned with getting on with the work and with discovering what *can* be done, rather than with lamenting that it will not bring us to the immediate solution of all our theological difficulties.

IV Notes on the Philosophical Anthropology of William James

If it is true that each generation of philosophers must discover its own truth in the history of philosophy, the work of philosophy itself cannot be carried on apart from the continual reappraisal, the continual re-evaluation of the philosophical history of which it is the living continuation. In American philosophy we are witnessing the beginnings of a radical reevaluation of the thought of William James and with it the discovery that James can be credited with more than the creation of a typically American philosophical "ism," and that his thought has a more fundamental meaning for the evolution of twentieth-century philosophy than even his most partisan followers have yet claimed for it.

There is a myth of William James. It can be called the "myth of pragmatism," and James himself must be credited (or blamed) in large part for its creation and subsequent growth. Pick up almost any history of philosophy, whether written in France, England, Germany or America, and look up the chapter on William James. Or turn to any of the more specialized studies of his thought published up to the Second World War in Europe, or, in this country, up to the present moment. What do we find? That William James is the *American philosopher* par excellence, the founder of a pragmatic American-frontier style of philosophy concerned with facing "hard reality," concerned with "what works," the "cash value" of ideas, in short, a philosophy of practical *doing*, congenitally hostile to the empty rationalisms and idealisms of Old Europe and centered instead on the pluralism of experience as opposed to the monism of metaphysical thought.[1] He is remembered, indeed, for launching several original theories (on emotions, on perception, on the theory of mind and experience), nearly all of which, however, he left in a vague and badly defined state under the programmatic cloaks of "pluralism," "radical empiricism," and "pragmatism." It is this last "ism" which gets the most attention and the embarrassments of the "pragmatic theory of truth" usually suffice to exhaust the interest not only of James's adversaries but of his disciples and friends as well.

As I have said, James himself must bear a major share of the blame for this development, since from the day that he launched his pragmatist platform at the University of California in 1898 he spent most of the rest of his philosophical career trying to win allies for it both within the academic world and among the general public. The popular style of his pragmatist essays, his lack of attention to the logic of his system, his partisanship on behalf of younger "pragmatist" friends like Dewey and Schiller, his ignorance of, or his unwillingness to meet, the serious objections of his opponents, show that he identified his own philosophical and emotional success with the fortunes of pragmatism. True, toward the end of his life, under the influence of Bergson and the promptings of his own conscience, he attempted to return to a more systematic philosophical elaboration of the foundational insights at the origin of this new philosophy. But the demands of his public as well as his increasing physical debility made it impossible for him to finish—or even fairly to begin—what was to have been his greatest philosophical work.[2]

The result has been the creation of the "myth of pragmatism." Whether we turn to John Dewey, Ralph Barton Perry, Horace Kallen, Sidney Hook, Morton White, or even Émile Boutroux, Emmanuel Leroux, or Jean Wahl, we find—in spite of important individual nuances to be sure—essentially the same picture of James's philosophical intentions and evolution. He was the founder of a pragmatism (whose central idea he borrowed from Charles Sanders Peirce) which, though fraught with logical and metaphysical difficulties, can be refined into a naturalistic philosophy of "instrumentalism" or "functionalism" which, if not ultimately acceptable, is at least a respectable, important, and *typically American* contribution to the plethora of systems which constitute the history of philosophy. Anything else James may have said, including even his "gross spiritualism,"[3] or his notion of the subconscious, for instance, can be properly incorporated within this framework.

I do not wish to contend that this myth of pragmatism, as the philosophy of William James, is completely false, much less that it is historically unjustified. James is a pragmatist: It is rather the *meaning* of his pragmatism which must be rescued from the oversimplified version of it uncritically accepted by historians of philosophy. By reducing James to his pragmatism we risk losing the authentic genius and originality of his thought. Within the last few years several studies of the thought of William James have been undertaken, chiefly by European philosophers under the influence of the phenomenology of Edmund Husserl, which have revealed that the prevailing account of James's thought is subject to considerable reinterpretation. These studies have been centered more around James's only finished systematic treatise, *The Principles of Psychology*, than around his later and more popular essays and lectures. This is not, however, a simple return to the *early James* (as we have recently returned to the "young Hegel" or the "young Marx") to oppose his youthful work to his later developments which would then be "interpreted" as gradual falsifications of originally sound insights. For, if it is true that *The Principles of Psychology* contains, at least in germinal form, all of James's most fundamental and original ideas, it is not true that this is a youthful work. It was twelve years in gestation and was published when James had reached the age of forty-nine, after long years of teaching and writing philosophy as well as empirical study and research. By the age of forty-nine some philosophers have already published a whole library of books; as for William James, he never again found the time or the self-discipline necessary to produce a sequel worthy of this *magnum opus*.[4] Moreover, it can perhaps be shown that James's later writings are in many respects only the clarification and development of philosophical positions established in the *Principles* and that they can best be understood in this light.

However this may be, the fact is that such philosophers as Aron Gurwitsch, Alfred Schutz, John Wild, Herbert Spiegelberg, and, more recently, Johannes Linschoten, have pointed out hitherto unrecognized elements in the philosophy of James which put his contribution to twentieth-century philosophy into an entirely new light.[5] At the very least it has been shown that the reputation of James as a philosopher no longer rests exclusively on the fate of the "pragmatic theory of truth," whatever the value and merits of that theory may be.

It is not my aim to recapitulate here the results of these recent studies, to discuss them in detail, or to criticize their validity. Indeed, the most recent among them goes so far in establishing parallels between the thought of James and that of Husserl that one instinctively feels that *some* of the evidence, at least, has been rigged.[6] Nevertheless these studies have shown that James and Husserl were working, or can be interpreted as working, in convergent directions. In common with the intentions of the early Vienna Circle and twentieth-century philosophy as a whole, we find in James and Husserl a common anti-metaphysical attitude, a desire to "dissolve" traditional metaphysical problems by *a return to experience*. At the same time James and Husserl (and Bergson) are distinguished from the logical positivists and from traditional empiricists (particularly the British empiricists) by a conception of experience as something much more complex, much more variegated, much more existential than that allowed by the purely "cognitive" (and "sensationalist") accounts of experience accepted by earlier empiricists. Further, James and Husserl conceived philosophy to be primarily concerned with the realm of *meaning* and they attempted in various ways to restate all philosophical problems in terms of meaning. This necessarily led them to place *man-the-experiencer* at the center of their philosophical preoccupation, to replace metaphysics, so to speak, with "philosophical anthropology."

For the purposes of the present paper I intend to leave it to historians of philosophy to assess the validity of the studies to which I have referred above, and to worry about whether or not we can legitimately speak of William James as a "phenomenologist." He did not use this term to describe his own work, and the Hegelian sound of the word would certainly have repelled him. Also, there are many fundamental differences which separate his own philosophical positions from those of Husserl. This paper, therefore, will not be a further contribution to the rapprochement between James's philosophy and the phenomenological tradition. It will be limited strictly to the thought of James himself with a view toward presenting a broadly schematic and highly synthetic view of his *philosophy of man*, his "philosophical anthropology," as the *natural center* and *focal point* of his thought. If I refer occasionally to James as a "phenomenologist" or call to mind certain parallels which have been pointed out between him and certain phenomenologists, I will also attempt to indicate briefly certain important points of divergence.

EXPERIENCE

William James was a philosopher of experience, an empiricist, but his empiricism is distinguished from that of earlier philosophy in that it is a *radical* empiricism. From his earlier writings, he protested against the atomistic-associationist theory of mind held by the classical British empiricists in favor of a conception of "pure experiences" as he called it. Whereas the doctrine of Hume was vitiated by a theory about the nature of sensations conceived independently of and prior to experience itself. James proposed a resolute return to "pure experience" as it is given in "the immediate flux of life" prior to any theory about it. He reproached Hume for not going far enough.

> To be radical, an empiricism must neither admit into its constructions any element that is not directly experienced, nor exclude from them any element that is directly experienced. For such a philosophy, the *relations that connect experience must themselves be experienced relations, and any kind of relation experienced must be accounted as "real" as anything else in the system.*[7]

The stream of consciousness is not composed only of "substantive parts" but also of "transitive parts"—not only of experiences designated by nouns, but of those designated by conjunctions, prepositions, adverbs, syntactic forms and inflections of voice as well.

> We ought to say a feeling of *and* a feeling of *if*, a feeling of *but*, and a feeling of *by*, quite as readily as we say a feeling of *blue* or a feeling of *cold*.[8]

The second element of James's criticism of Hume and classical empiricism is directed against its *phenomenalism*. Though James himself has frequently been accused of phenomenalism,[9] he is innocent of the charge, at least if we can interpret some of his more unfortunate formulations in the light of his clearer statements of his position. It is here that the phenomenologist most regrets that James had not read Husserl and that he had no fully developed conception of the intentionality of consciousness.[10] But James does clearly reject all "mind-stuff" theories according to which what we experience immediately and directly are not the objects of the real world but only our own subjective stream of consciousness (however complex and structured it may be). James agreed with Peirce that "we do not experience our experiences, but we experience the object as such."[11] His essential distinction is that between the *object* and the *object-known-as*.

> The object of every thought, then, is neither more nor less than all that the thought thinks, exactly as the thought thinks it, however symbolic the manner of the thinking may be.[12]

I know the real *object*, but only as experienced by me. This is clearly no Kantian distinction between *phenomenon* and *Ding-an-sich*, a device James repeatedly rejects. There is no *Ding-an-sich*, says James; what we experience *are* the things themselves and our experience is therefore intrinsically referential or "intentional" in the phenomenological sense of the term. "Human thought . . . deals with objects independent of itself,"[13] but it necessarily deals with these objects *as experienced*. The *object-known-as* is still the *object* of the real world, it is not a *tertium quid*, but our actual, experiential contact with the real.

On this basis we can distinguish James not only from Hume and Kant but from Mach and Husserl as well. There are passages in James which sound very much like Mach, as when he states, for example, that "the percept is the reality," and that "pure experience" and "the world" are interchangeable terms. But, unlike Mach, James does not erect his radical empiricism into a metaphysics or go to the extreme of saying that material objects are *nothing* but the sums of spatial and temporal sensations, etc.[14] James is not an empirio-criticist but an *intuitionist* and what is *given* in intuitive experience is the *real* world. Intuition or experience, he says, is the *point of intersection* of consciousness and reality. James's philosophy, in short, does not justify any attempt to reconstruct reality with the materials of perception alone. At the same time James is clearly not a full Husserlian, though his theory of experience seems closer to Husserlian phenomenology than to any other contemporary theory. Like Husserl he distinguishes *that which* is presented to consciousness (the *object-known-as*) and the *occurrence* of the presentation. Consciousness itself is an ever-moving stream, it never has the *same* experience twice. What remains the *same* in a series of experiences of a given object is the *real object* itself, that reality toward which our ceaselessly flowing, ever-temporal consciousness is directed, and which can be identified through a series of perceptual acts none of which are numerically or even qualitatively identical. But just here, where James seems so close to Husserl, he also seems farther away.[15] For James, it is not merely *the object as meant*, the fully idealized *noema*, which remains the *same* through a series of different experiences of it (or as experienced by other minds, from other viewpoints), but rather the *real*, existing, historical object itself in the world.

Must we therefore say that James remains on the side of "realism" versus "idealism," or is he not rather, like Husserl, also searching for a way out of this sterile impasse, for a theory of experience which will be neither realistic nor idealistic but phenomenological? If we follow the most profound intentions of James's thought, this would seem to be the case. As Ralph Barton Perry has pointed out, with great penetration, the philosophy of James is neither a philosophy of objects and actions nor a philosophy of ideas; it is a philosophy of the *experience* of objects and actions *in which the subject itself is a participant*.[16] The root of James's pragmatism lies here. The perceptual-active level of experience (what James calls "pure" experience, what Merleau-Ponty calls "sensory-motor perception") is more fundamental than the level of ideas and fully reflexive thought. James wishes to establish a philosophy of experience which can get beneath the "natural selection of thought," to recover "the original plenum of existence." But this "original plenum" is not an unstructured, chaotic mass of discrete impressions—though James sometimes speaks as if it were. It is the "field of original meanings" from which all ideas and intellectual constructions are derived and in which they are founded.[17]

REALITY

The consequences of *radical empiricism* are very important not only for philosophy as an academic discipline but for the activity of the philosopher himself. For, in a radically empiricist framework, "nothing shall be admitted as a fact . . . except what can be experienced at some definite time and by some experiencer. . . . Everything real must be experienceable somewhere and every kind of thing experienced must somewhere be real."[18] James, no less than Husserl, no less than the logical positivists and their successors, places philosophy completely outside speculative metaphysics. The very category of *reality* thus becomes problematic, and James solves it in an essentially phenomenological direction.

First of all, all organization of experience, according to James, is due to the "selective interest" and the "selective activity" of the experiencer. This experiential and active selection brings about differentiations, discriminations, and objectifications in function of the practical interests and the pragmatic needs of the experiencer. The result of these "objectifications" is the experienced life-world. (This "selective interest" need not be understood in any fully reflexive sense—but rather and primarily in the sense of the pre-reflexively felt needs, goals, and intentions of *homo faber*.) As Aron Gurwitsch says, James has "a teleological conception of the human mind."[19] Reality is *that which* is experienced. James gives this definition its full weight: Reality itself is strictly correlative to our experience of it. It is *capable* of being experienced and *in so far forth* it can be known. Moreover, our experience of reality is historical and always growing. Consciousness itself is "cumulative." Nobody can foresee what the future may hold, what new aspects of reality remain to be revealed in experience. "Our science is a drop, our ignorance a sea."[20] All knowledge of reality depends on human activity and *reality* itself can be approached and defined only through experience.

The word "reality," says James, signifies *"simply a relation to our emotional and active life . . . whatever excites and stimulates our interest is real,"* and to that extent.[21] In an extremely dense passage James writes:

> *The fons et origo of all reality, whether from the absolute or the practical point of view, is thus subjective, is ourselves.* . . . Reality, starting from our Ego, thus sheds itself from point to point—first, upon all objects which have an immediate sting of interest for our Ego in them, and next, upon the objects most continuously related with these. . . .

> These are our *living* realities. . . .

> We reach thus the important conclusion that *our own reality, that sense of our own life which we at every moment possess, is the ultimate of ultimates for our belief.* . . . The world of living realities as contrasted with unrealities is thus anchored in the Ego, considered as an active and emotional term.[22]

It is doubtful whether any empirical philosophy has ever stated the strict correlativity of the Ego and the World more strongly. When Merleau-Ponty calls man-the-experiencer the "absolute source" of the world—a statement for which he has been recently reproached—it is in this Jamesian sense.[23] Like Augustine, like Erigena, like Descartes, like Husserl, James turns to *the experience of oneself experiencing* as the fundamental fact, the starting point for philosophy (the *Urtatsache*, said Husserl). However, it is not the Ego *as thinker* or the Ego as *pure cognition, pure consciousness,* which James has in mind, and in this he is distinguished from Descartes and, to a more qualified extent, from Husserl. It is the *acting Ego,* the Ego considered as "an active and emotional term." Here we find the second root of James's pragmatism, a more fundamental one, and we see to what extent even a radical empiricism is also necessarily a metaphysics—a metaphysics of experience.

Aron Gurwitsch and Alfred Schutz have followed James in further clarifying and distinguishing the various *orders of reality* ("sub-universes" in James's terminology) which can be developed on the basis of this experiential definition of the real. It is not necessary to recapitulate their work here; rather I will restrict myself to emphasizing what James, on the basis of this definition, declares to be the *paramount reality*, namely, the world of perception or the "world of sense" as he called it. By the "world of sense" James does *not* mean the chaotic mass of dumb "stimuli" of physiological or "sensationalistic" psychology, but the concretely experienced "life-world" to which Merleau-Ponty, for his part, accords "the primacy of perception." This world, says James, is the *paramount reality* from which the worlds of imagination, of dreaming, of all idealities, of mathematical and logical thought, even the worlds of science, philosophy and religion, are derived. Two conclusions follow immediately from this thesis. If the perceptual world is the primary reality, the structures of categorial thought are necessarily rooted in the pre-reflexive contact with reality which we call *perception*. Reason and categorial thought are not prior to experience as Kant would have it; they reflect rather than determine the structures of perceptual experience. "Apprehension" flows from "prehension." We can see what such a notion of reality means for the traditional problems of metaphysics. Being, the *really real*, is *this experienced world itself*, and human activity is the source of all order, of all structure, of all meaning in Being. Second, it follows, and this is essential for any full account of James's later "pragmatism," that all theoretical curiosity, all "philosophical" activity, follows upon and begins from the practical demands of pre-categorial, pre-thematic, practical-perceptual life in the world. This finite, unfinished, historical world of experience must itself "breast non-entity" and be "self-supporting."[24]

REASON AND BELIEF

One of the points at which William James is most indebted to Hume is in his *notion of belief* and in the priority of practical belief over all other forms of "knowledge." In one of his earliest philosophical writings, "The Sentiment of Rationality" (1880), James provides us with a veritable *phenomenology*, not of reason, but *of rationality*. His question is: what precisely is the *experience* of rationality? His answers to this question contain in germ the whole "epistemology" of pragmatism and the essential ideas of his later "pragmatic theory of truth." The "will to believe" is not a *right*, like my right to a fair trial under the constitution;[25] it is a fundamental structure of life with respect to which alone it is possible to pose the derived question of the rational justification of any particular given beliefs.

The feeling of rationality (i.e., belief) is defined as "a feeling of the sufficiency of the present moment, of its absoluteness—the absence of all need to explain it, account for it or justify it."[26] It is the point at which we cease asking questions, at which we are at ease, at peace, at rest in our (implicit or explicit) present view of things. Normally, it is the taken-for-grantedness of the world and of our lives; the very precarious state of equilibrium of intellectual and emotional repose in which we remain until the next question is posed, until our state of belief is challenged or begins again to cause us perplexity. The point at which men, and philosophers, are willing to cease questioning, to accept explanations as provisionally "ultimate," differs in function of the practical or theoretical problems with which they are faced. Normally, we "believe as much as we can" and alter our beliefs as little as possible and only to the extent forced upon us by circumstances, by novelty, surprise, the threat of irrationality.[27] But however far we push our effort of rationalizing our practical and theoretical beliefs, the point at which we must cut off, and say "it is sufficient," is *always* arbitrary. Each man, and each philosopher, approaches reality from his own point of view, from his own experience, and an explanation which for Hegel was fully satisfying will no longer satisfy his disciples. "The uneasiness which keeps the never-resting clock of metaphysics in motion, is the consciousness that the non-existence of this world is just as possible as its existence."[28]

In short, we must always stop somewhere and rest in *belief*. But what is it which makes one belief more satisfactory than another? James answers that it is the extent to which it, at least provisionally, tends "to legitimate our tendencies"—our most profound, multi-layered, completely motivated, personal needs, aims, goals, desires. It is on this basis that James distinguishes "serious" philosophies, like his own, from "anaesthetic" philosophies like those of Schopenhauer, Hartmann, Spencer, or the Stoics, who make renunciation and acquiescence in the present a rule of life. The intellect, reason, for James is entirely "built up of practical interests" and even in its most theoretical activities it involves the "philosophic craving to have expectancy defined," to go beyond partial and unacceptable theories, to search out new obstacles, to ask new questions, to "press against" the present state of affairs so that a *better* state and more adequate beliefs may be achieved. Man, according to James, is a future-oriented, dynamic striving, a process which is a *praxis*. But James's *meliorism* (and here we see the ethical as well as the epistemological aspect of *belief*) does not involve the necessary conviction that a total rational synthesis is possible in the more or less distant future, that human striving will some day be finished and come to a perfect end. A philosophy of experience can tell us nothing of such "ultimate reality." It can only tell us that the world is going on, that we do not know what the outcome of history will be, that science and knowledge *can* advance, but that we have no guarantee that our present state is in advance or in retreat. We *believe* that we can make the world better, that, if we do nothing, it will probably get worse, and therefore the whole of our intellectual and moral energy involves a striving toward the future, not, as in popular existentialism, a *blind* striving, because we do have light, but a striving fraught with risk, the need to choose without full knowledge of the consequences of our actions, the need to *believe* in order one day to *know*, since belief *may* bring into existence its own object.

James is at his best when he is giving us examples of how belief stimulates action and makes what was *not yet* true become a living reality and a social force in our lives. Unlike many of our contemporaries James has no fear of rhetorical arguments. He knows too well that philosophical belief—like all beliefs—is created and "justified" not by impersonal, "objective" observations, but by decisions to act, to choose, if necessary, *against the evidence*. Epistemologically he is anti-Aristotelian and anti-positivistic. The positivists invite us to be "passive observers" of the world, to remain in eternal ignorance or agnosticism, to suspend belief in order to see more clearly. They do not see, says James, that *evidence* is not given, it must be created. All evidence is ambiguous and equivocal, in need of interpretation. All our scientific laws are only a kind of "conceptual shorthand" and not a reading of the eternal mind of God. Knowledge is not the work of passively copying reality or receiving "representations" of it; it is also, and primarily, a "way of getting into fruitful relations with reality."[29] Up to now, James writes, philosophers and scientists have believed that truth lies *in rebus* to be discovered there. But this is itself a belief which has no "a priori" probability at all and which seems extremely unlikely the more it is thought about.

> If . . . we assume God to have thought in advance of every *possible* flight of human fancy . . . his mind becomes too much like a Hindoo idol with

three heads, eight arms and six breasts, too much made up of super-foetation and redundancy for us to wish to copy it, and the whole notion of copying tends to evaporate from . . . sciences.[30]

James opts for the opposite "belief" as a more "fruitful" one. After Heisenberg, after Bohr, after Gödel, this direction of James's thought does not cause us the difficulties it caused his contemporaries and we begin to see that James, too, can be called an "existentialist." But we cannot go further into the problems of pragmatist epistemology here, our only purpose is to pull together some of the main themes of James's thought and to show how they both flow from and converge toward a view of man as a radically individual, unified, behaving and experiencing organism in the world. We believe that this view of man as an *active experiencer* is the central idea of James's philosophy around which his theory of consciousness, his theory of reality, his theory of knowledge, his pragmatism, his ethics, and his philosophy of religion can be organized and brought into their correct "phenomenological" focus.

THE SELF

As on some of the other Jamesian themes we have alluded to, recent studies on the phenomenology of the self have tended to show how far James was ahead of his time in the simple and yet profoundly modern psychological descriptions he gave of the *experience of the self*.[31] In his chapter on "The Consciousness of Self" in the *Principles of Psychology* he adopts a simple framework centered around the distinction between the *experienced* (or, in his words, "empirical") *selves* and the *experiencing self*. He pointed out that there is not *one self*, but that there are *many selves* (the material, the social, the spiritual, and so on) and that we identify and dissociate ourselves with these various "selves" and their several aspects in function of our various and changing interests, intentions, and life-situations. In short, what we, in ordinary language, call the "self" is not the experiencing ego at all, but one or the other of its various objects, one of its objectifications, with which we are free to identify or dissociate ourselves to a greater or lesser extent, depending on many highly complex emotional, motivational, and behavioral attitudes which are continually changing and evolving.

The more fundamental question involves asking *who* it is who identifies himself in varying degrees with these diverse "empirical" or "objective" selves. And here James meets one of his most fundamental "phenomenological" problems: the problem which Sartre faces in "The Transcendence of the Ego," which Merleau-Ponty discusses under the "lived Body," which Gilbert Ryle puzzles over in his chapter on the "Systematic Elusiveness of the I," and which divides phenomenologists into "egologists" like Husserl and "non-egologists" like Gurwitsch. In the *Principles of Psychology* James's position is hesitant. On the one hand he clearly sees that the "self of selves," the innermost I, the *experiencer* par excellence, cannot be distinguished in a Cartesian and Kantian sense from the "bodily self"—from the "collection of these particular notions in the head or between the head and the throat" (!) which accompany and condition all my conscious and experiential states.[32] The ego cannot be a *"pure ego"* but must be "my historic Me, a collection of objective facts."[33]

Yet, we do *experience* our personal identity both as bodies ("we feel the whole cubic mass of our body all the while, it gives us an unceasing sense of personal existence"[34]) and as "the pure activity of our thought taking place as such." All men instinctively divide the world into the *me* and the *not-me*[35]—not only in the sense of the *me* which is the object of fully reflexive thought but in the sense of the *me* which is the continually experienced *I* and which constitutes my personal identity. James holds that "every thought is *owned*" and that the only consciousness we can experience is that of a *personal* consciousness.[36] But James does not understand this personal *me* in any "substantialistic" sense. Consciousness is a "cumulative" stream or process of awareness; it is the continual "self-appropriation" of its own activities; each "pulse of consciousness" claims and "owns" each preceding pulse and "identifies" it as a previous section of its own "stream." Consciousness is never the *same* at any two moments of its temporal development because it is always *more than* and *different from* what it was, and yet it is the *same consciousness* which continually "appropriates" its past and becomes cumulatively different at each moment of its evolution.

James is clearest about what he rejects: the theory of the substantial soul, the associationistic theory of Hume, the Transcendental Ego of Kant—all of which are rejected on "phenomenological" grounds, i.e., as unsatisfactory accounts of our *experience* of self-identity. But on the relationship of the bodily processes to the "self" which is "never an object to itself"[37] James gives, in *The Principles,* no clear answer and seems to hesitate between parallelism, epiphenomenalism, and interactionism, depending on his polemical concerns of the moment. He was content to leave the problem open and unsolved.

Later, he came back to this question in the famous essay "Does Consciousness Exist?" and elsewhere in the *Essays on Radical Empiricism*. But, here again, he does not overcome the original ambiguity; he can be read as an "egologist" or as a "non-egologist" (though I believe the egological interpretation is more consonant with the tenor of his philosophy as a whole, particularly since he continues to speak elsewhere of the *experiencing ego* as a unified "self" up to the end of his life). In "Does Consciousness Exist?" he states that *pure consciousness* is "the name of a nonentity" because, ultimately, it *cannot be experienced*. The experiencing ego is always ahead of itself; at the moment it is experiencing it is itself not-yet-experienced. It cannot be objectified because it is the *objectifier*. And for this reason, James claims—on the surest phenomenological grounds—that it does not exist as an *entity*, as a thing among things. But, clearly, it does exist, he admits, as a *function* (or a process).

> There is . . . no aboriginal stuff or quality of being, contrasted with that of which material objects are made, and of which our thoughts of them are made, but there is a function in experience which thoughts perform, and for the performance of which this quality of being is involved. The function is *knowing*.[38]

Consciousness *as a function* is prior to the dichotomy of subject and object; it is "subjective and objective both at once"; it is "entirely impersonal . . . pure experience." One feels that what James primarily lacked for a more adequate solution to this problem was precisely the Husserlian and Sartrean distinction between the pre-reflexive (pre-personal, not-yet-reflected) consciousness and the fully reflexive, judging consciousness. Phenomenally the *I* appears as object *only* on the fully reflexive level, but this does not exclude its presence *as subject* even in pre-reflexive experience. However, it is clear that we can attribute to James an "egological" theory of consciousness only on the basis of an "interpretation" of his thought as a whole, and not on the basis of what he explicitly says himself on the subject of the ego. This very fact is itself, however, most instructive. James did not believe in systems, but in the description of experience. If there are impasses and even contradictions in his thought, it is because he never wanted to go beyond the experiential evidence of his assertions, because of his faithfulness to his program of radical empiricism. This very fact tends to confirm rather than infirm the thesis of those who now see James as at least a "proto-phenomenologist."

ACTION

We have, up to now, circled around James's philosophy of man by moving from his notion of experience to that of reality, to reason and belief, to the problem of the self and now finally to the most fundamental and basic category, the one which lies beneath all the others and which is closest to the center of his thought: the *category* of *action*, understood primarily as the *individual action* of a unified behaving human organism in the world. This is the distinctive point of view from which James approached reality and which, we believe, ultimately motivated his philosophical positions, an idea he worked out in several distinctive ways in the multiple and diverse theories he proposed and defended. It is not contended that this idea was ever rendered fully explicit in his thought or that he worked it out with complete logical rigor in all its ramifications, that he did not occasionally adopt positions which were very imperfectly reconcilable with his central intention and with what he ultimately meant to say. But I believe it is by focusing on *action* as the central category of James's thought that we can best unify his insights, and justify the claim that his philosophy is above all else "philosophical anthropology."

It is impossible to do more here than to indicate briefly in what way this conception of *action* is central for William James and the argument I will use here will be biographical.[39] We have already shown that James's thought has some themes in common with existential philosophy; there is another, more important, similarity, namely, in the fact that James philosophized not only on the basis of *life*, but on the basis *of his own life*, his own personal experience. He was not a detached, disinterested *Zuschauer*, but a man passionately involved in the philosophical questions he took up. If a philosophical question had no *personal* importance for him, James simply ignored it.

We know that the gravest crisis of his own personal emotional and intellectual development was what he called his crisis *of freedom*. We know, further, that in his twenty-seventh year, after a period of great depression and melancholy (which frequently took "the form of panic fear" for his own sanity), James experienced "a horrible fear of my own existence," as he wrote, and thought more than once of taking his own life. Finally, we know that the cause of this crisis was not merely physiological but that it took the form of an obsessive psychological preoccupation with the problem of freedom versus determinism. He had studied chemistry and medicine and was prosecuting studies in physiological psychology which convinced him intellectually that he could be a "completely determined" being. The scientific evidence for this appeared to him overwhelming and was the cause of an intolerable psychological oppression, for James *experienced* himself phenomenally—in spite of all the scientific evidence—to be a free man. For James freedom thus came to mean the *deliberate achievement* of the ability *to act:* on himself, on others, on the world. His ultimate liberation came neither from medicine nor in the form of special philosophical reasons for believing himself to be free, but in his own decision *to act*. Action, in the philosophy of James, is another word for *Freedom*. By the decision to act he became a philosopher and the philosophy he developed is a philosophy of the *free act*.[40]

His account of this is well known but worth repeating. At the time he lived through the last stages of his emotional and philosophical crisis he was reading Renouvier.

> I think that yesterday was a crisis in my life [he wrote]. I finished the first part of Renouvier's second *Essais* and see no reason why his definition of Free Will—"the sustaining of a thought *because* I *choose* to when I might have other thoughts"—need be the definition of an illusion. At any rate, I will assume for the present . . . that it is no illusion. My first act of free will shall be to believe in free will.[41]

When, much later, James wrote an essay on the question "Is Life Worth Living?" he answered typically: "It depends on the *liver*." James had *cured himself* of his gloomy thoughts of suicide by *the decision to act freely*, and it is in this experience, rather than in the contemplation of "life on the nineteenth-century American frontier," that we should seek the root and inspiration of his later philosophical development. James was a philosopher who always opted for the "livelier" hypothesis, who avoided "anaesthetic" solutions, who avoided any fixed positions which would "block inquiry," who kept his mind open to all kinds and all realms of experience, who was, in short, a *radical empiricist*, because of an *experience* and an *ideal;* namely, that man is *free to act*, i.e., to create both truth and history.

Notes

1. J. N. Mohanty, *Husserl and Frege* (Bloomington: Indiana University Press, 1982).

2. Personally, I think that one of the better is to be found in an unjustly neglected book by E. C. Moore, *The American Pragmatists: Peirce, James, Dewey* (New York: Columbia University Press, 1961). It is at least one which is nuanced and which comes close to answering the most obvious objections to hasty formulations of the theory.

3. We must be very careful here. We must remind every reader of James of the culminating Chapter XXVIII of the *Principles* on "Necessary Truths" in their relationship to perception and other intuitional forms of experience, a chapter which had a certain impact on Husserl and which James himself never forgot either. Here the distinction between truths of reason (or language and logic) and truths of fact is fully explained, endorsed and defended at great length. I deal with this in Chapter I below.

4. Richard Rorty, *Philosophy and the Mirror of Nature* (Princeton: Princeton University Press, 1979). Another of Richard Rorty's recent publications I have had in mind and which is contributing to a rebirth of interest in American Pragmatism is his *Consequences of Pragmatism* (Minneapolis: University of Minnesota Press, 1982), a collection of his essays from 1972–1980, and also his contribution to Peter Caws, ed., *Two Centuries of Philosophy in America* (Totowa, N.J.: Rowman and Littlefield, 1980). Rorty's contribution is entitled: "Genteel Syntheses, Professional Analyses, Transcendentalist Culture," pp. 228–39, where pride of place goes to Santayana. This is a collection in honor of America's bicentennial. In my own view by far the best essay in this book is that by T. L. S. Sprigge, "The Distinctiveness of American Philosophy," pp. 199–214.

5. In my view Rorty's book should be read in the light of J. N. Mohanty's review in the *Journal of the British Society for Phenomenology* 14, Jan. 1983, pp. 91–98. Rorty's book, of course received a *lot* of reviews, including two by serious philosophers who raise some objections (namely, Charles Taylor in the *Times Literary Supplement*, December 26, 1980, and

Quentin Skinner in *The New York Review of Books*, March 19, 1981), but even these are mainly so eager to praise and so close to the subject that they seem to lack a good deal of objectivity. Mohanty's review, by contrast, reflects the objectivity of a Sanskrit philologian as well as a continentally trained philosopher.

6. William James, *The Varieties of Religious Experience* (New York: Mentor Books, 1958), p. 47.

7. William James, *The Principles of Psychology* (New York: Dover, 1950), p. 649.

8. As cited by Ralph Barton Perry, *In the Spirit of William James* (Bloomington: Indiana University Press, 1958), p. 58. It was at that time otherwise unpublished; I do not know if it may be published or has been published elsewhere since.

9. One of the rather timid points Quentin Skinner makes in his review of Rorty's *Philosophy and the Mirror of Nature* is that Rorty should have given a larger place and some real attention to the work of R. G. Collingwood. In his *Speculum Mentis* of 1924 Collingwood had argued against, and in his 1940 *Essay on Metaphysics* he had "repudiated," indubitable foundations of thought because, according to Skinner, the presuppositions of each science are given to it in a determined historical framework which the individual science cannot and does not question. Thus there are no "ultimate categories." This, of course is balderdash, and I hope Collingwood, whom I otherwise highly esteem, did not say that. Aristotle (and his disciple, Aquinas) would put it differently. It is true that no particular science can defend its own first principles; these are *for it* matters of faith or belief (perhaps almost in Hume's sense or Montaigne's or even Santayana's), but there is a form of investigation which does just that, namely, to investigate the presuppositions which other sciences—like geometry, said Aristotle; like theology, said Aquinas—take for granted. And that is the work of reason, of philosophy. It is in this sense that Aristotle says sciences like geometry, optics, etc., are "subordinate" to metaphysics, namely, because they take their first principles, uncriticized, from metaphysics, whereas metaphysics establishes its own absolute first principles.

10. *Principles*, pp. 677–78.

I. Necessary Truth and Perception: William James on the Structure of Experience

1. Apart from the papers at the present symposium, "William James and the Structure of the Self," by Robert R. Ehman, and "William James and the Phenomenology of Belief," by John Wild, one could recall "William James and Existential Authenticity," by John Wild, in *The Journal of Existentialism*, Spring 1965, pp. 243–56; "Notes on the Philosophical Anthropology of William James," by James M. Edie, in *An Invitation to Phenomenology*

(Chicago: Quadrangle Books, 1965), pp. 110–32; and above all, Johannes Linschoten, *Auf dem Weg zu einer phänomenologischen Psychologie, Die Psychologie von William James* (Berlin: Walter de Gruyter, 1961). Bruce Wilshire read a further contribution, entitled "The Phenomenological Breakthrough in the Psychology of William James," at the meeting of the American Philosophical Association held in December 1967.

2. Maurice Merleau-Ponty, *The Primacy of Perception and Other Essays*, ed. James M. Edie (Evanston, Ill.: Northwestern University Press, 1964), pp. 19–20.

3. Ibid., p. 8.

4. I am here taking for granted the methodological conclusions of "Notes on the Philosophical Anthropology of William James," and of an article entitled "William James and the Phenomenology of Religious Experience," in *American Philosophy and the Future*, ed. Michael Novak (New York: Scribner's, 1968), pp. 247ff.

5. Edmund Husserl, *Ideas*, tr. W. R. Boyce Gibson (New York: Macmillan, 1931), p. 86.

6. Merleau-Ponty, *The Primacy of Perception*, p. 50.

7. William James, *The Principles of Psychology* (New York: Dover, 1950), vol. 2, p. 299.

8. Erwin Straus, *The Primary World of Senses: A Vindication of Sensory Experience* (New York: The Free Press, 1963).

9. Alfred Schutz, "On Multiple Realities," in *Collected Papers* (The Hague: Nijhoff, 1962), vol. 1, pp. 207ff.

10. Aron Gurwitsch, *The Field of Consciousness* (Pittsburgh: Duquesne University Press, 1964), pp. 410ff. At this place Gurwitsch recalls Aristotle's doctrine of the analogy of "being" (without adopting its metaphysical implications) to indicate the kind of *metabasis eis allo genus* involved in speaking of the various "orders of existence" correlative to the perceptual, imaginative, fictive, and idealizing intentions of consciousness respectively. If one wanted to pursue historical parallels, it would be interesting to note that Husserl also spoke of "truth" and "being" as being both "categories" in the same sense and as being correlative (*Logische Untersuchungen*, Erster Band, "Prolegomena" [Halle: Niemeyer, 1928.] p. 228 [cf. Marvin Farber, *The Foundation of Phenomenology* (New York: Paine-Whittman, 1962), p. 124]). This sounds a little like the Aristotle of the Ninth Book of the *Metaphysics*, for whom "being" or "existence" was not a univocal category. *Tò ón polachos legetai*, the term "being" is predicated in many different senses, and the primary sense belongs to the *ousiai* of perceptual experience within the real world.

11. James, *Principles*, vol. 2, pp. 296–98.

12. Ibid., p. 306.

13. Cf. Gurwitsch, *The Field of Consciousness*, p. 418.

14. Cf. Maurice Natanson, "Man as an Actor," a paper read at the Second Lexington Conference on "Phenomenology of Will and Action," held at

Lexington, Kentucky, May 15, 1964. In these remarks I am here repeating some observations I made originally in reply to Natanson's paper.

15. Husserl discusses the founding of categorial acts primarily in the *Sixth Investigation* and in *Erfahrung und Urteil*, though this theme is a constant throughout his writings, as in the first chapter of *Ideas*, which would be unintelligible without it. Merleau-Ponty comes back to this theme very frequently in his writings, but perhaps the most explicit texts are to be found in "The Primacy of Perception" and in "Phenomenology and the Sciences of Man," both included in *The Primacy of Perception*.

16. *Logische Untersuchungen*, Zweiter Band, I, Teil, p. 208.

17. James, *Principles*, vol. 1, pp. 145ff., 196, 235–36ff.

18. Gurwitsch, *The Field of Consciousness*, p. 168.

19. James, *Principles*, vol. 1, pp. 230–31.

20. Ibid., p. 236, transposed.

21. Gurwitsch, *The Field of Consciousness*, has analyzed James's contributions to the phenomenological theory of consciousness in considerable detail, treating of his doctrines of "sensible totals," pp. 25ff.; his concept of the "object of thought," pp. 184ff.; his theory of the "fringes" of consciousness, pp. 309ff.; etc.

22. James, *Principles*, vol. 2, p. 639.

23. Ibid., p. 633.

24. Ibid., pp. 620–21ff.

25. Ibid., pp. 641–42, 643–44.

26. Ibid., p. 637, note.

27. Ibid., p. 677.

28. Ibid., p. 649.

29. Ibid., p. 661.

30. James, *Essays in Radical Empiricism* (New York: Longmans, Green Co., 1942), p. 42; *The Will to Believe* (New York: Dover, 1956), p. 86. We are not here concerned with James's physiological studies or with his account of how the possibility of categorial thought might be accounted for on the basis of "mutations" in brain structures, since this part of the work is logically independent of his "phenomenological" reflections—as he himself recognizes.

31. Note that we are not here posing the question of the ontological status of such "entities." We are considering them only phenomenologically, i.e., as noematic orders of experience.

32. Merleau-Ponty, *The Primacy of Perception*, p. 25.

33. James, *Principles*, vol. 2, p. 335.

34. Ibid., p. 333.

35. Cf. Ralph Barton Perry, *In the Spirit of William James* (Bloomington: Indiana University Press, 1958), p. 49.

36. James, *Principles*, vol. 2, p. 634.

37. Ibid., p. 635, note.

38. Ibid., p. 652.
39. Ibid., p. 677.

II. William James and Phenomenology

This essay (first published in 1970) was inspired by the appearance of three new books on William James—Hans Linschoten, *On the Way Toward a Phenomenological Psychology, The Psychology of William James*, tr. Amedeo Giorgi (Pittsburgh: Duquesne University Press, 1968); Bruce Wilshire, *William James and Phenomenology: A Study of 'The Principles of Psychology'* (Bloomington: Indiana University Press, 1968); and John Wild, *The Radical Empiricism of William James* (New York: Doubleday, 1969)—in the context of the recently begun and growing phenomenological interpretation of his thought. See note 8 below.

1. See *The Writings of William James*, ed. John J. McDermott (New York: Random House, 1967), p. xvii.

2. Josiah Royce, *William James and Other Essays on the Philosophy of Life* (New York: Macmillan, 1911), p. 7.

3. Cited in Herbert Spiegelberg, *The Phenomenological Movement* (The Hague: Nijhoff, 1960), vol. 1, pp. 111–12. Cf. Ralph Barton Perry, *The Thought and Character of William James* (Boston: Little, Brown, 1935), vol. 2, p. 185: "The frequency with which a man loves to use the words *streng wissenschaftlich* is beginning to be for me a measure of the shallowness of his sense of truth. Altogether, the less we have to say about *Strenge* the better. . . ."

4. *The Letters of William James*, ed. Henry James (Boston: Atlantic Monthly Press, 1920), vol. 1, pp. 263–64. In another place James remarks on the "terrible flavor of humbug" about all of Wundt's writing (Perry, *Thought and Character*, vol. 2, pp. 55, 181). Even when he recognizes his indebtedness to his German sources in psychology, James always tempers his enthusiasm: "Within a few years what one may call a microscopic psychology has arisen in Germany. . . . This method taxes patience to the utmost, and could hardly have arisen in a country whose natives could be bored. Such Germans as Weber, Fechner, Vierordt, and Wundt obviously cannot. . . . The simple and open method of attack having done what it can, the method of patience, starving out, and harassing to death is tried; the Mind must submit to a regular *siege*, in which minute advantages gained night and day by the forces that hem her in must sum themselves up at last into her overthrow. There is little of the grand style about these new prism, pendulum, and chronograph-philosophers. They mean business, not chivalry" (*The Principles of Psychology* [New York: Dover, 1950], vol. 1, pp. 192–93). Of Fechner he wrote: "Fechner himself indeed was a German *Gelehrter* of the ideal type. . . . But it would be terrible if even such a dear old man as this could saddle our Sci-

ence forever with his patient whimsies, and, in a world so full of more nutritious objects of attention, compel all future students to plough through the difficulties, not only of his own works, but of the still drier ones written in his refutation. Those who desire this dreadful literature can find it; it has a 'disciplinary value'; but I will not even enumerate it in a footnote" (*Principles*, vol. 1, p. 549). To Stumpf he wrote: "The thought . . . of psycho-physical experimentation, and altogether of brass-instrument and algebraic-formula psychology fills me with horror" (Perry, *Thought and Character*, vol. 2, p. 195). And to Flournoy: "The results that come from all this laboratory work seem to me to grow more and more disappointing and trivial. What is most needed is new ideas. For every man who has one of them, one may find a hundred who are willing to drudge patiently at some unimportant experiment" (*Letters*, vol. 2, p. 54).

5. Bruce Wilshire, *William James and Phenomenology*, p. 239.

6. *Principles*, vol. 2, p. 661. In another place he wrote: "Kant's mind is the rarest and most intricate of all possible antique bric-a-brac museums, and connoisseurs and dilettanti will always wish to visit it and see the wondrous and racy contents. The temper of the dear old man about his work is perfectly detectable. And yet he is really—although I shrink with some terror from saying such a thing before some of you here present—at bottom a mere curio, a 'specimen'. . . . The true line of philosophic progress lies, in short, it seems to me, not so much *through* Kant as *round* him . . ." ("Philosophical Conceptions and Practical Results," *Writings*, p. 361.)

7. *Principles*, vol. 1, pp. 365–66. Since most of the direct quotations from James in this article will be from the *Principles*, we will henceforth refer to them by giving the volume and page number in parentheses in the body of the text. We will refer to the books by Linschoten, Wilshire, and Wild in the same manner when this can be done without ambiguity.

8. The principal contributions to this literature are, in chronological order, the following:

1) Alfred Schutz, "William James' Concept of the Stream of Thought Phenomenologically Interpreted," *Philosophy and Phenomenological Research* 1, 1941; reprinted in Alfred Schutz, *Collected Papers* (The Hague: Nijhoff, 1966), vol. 3, pp. 1–14.

2) Aron Gurwitsch, "William James' Theory of the 'Transitive Parts' of the Stream of Consciousness," *Philosophy and Phenomenological Research* 3, 1943; reprinted in Aron Gurwitsch, *Studies in Phenomenology and Psychology* (Evanston: Northwestern University Press, 1966), pp. 301–31.

3) Alfred Schutz, "On Multiple Realities," *Philosophy and Phenomenological Research* 5, 1945; reprinted in Schutz, *Collected Papers*, vol. 1, pp. 207–59.

4) Aron Gurwitsch, "On the Object of Thought," *Philosophy and Phenomenological Research* 7, 1947; reprinted in *Studies in Phenomenology and Psychology*, pp. 141–47.

5) Aron Gurwitsch, *La Théorie du champ de la conscience* (Paris: Desdée de Brouwer, 1957); English translation, *The Field of Consciousness* (Pittsburgh: Duquesne University Press, 1964).

6) Herbert Spiegelberg, *The Phenomenological Movement* (The Hague: Nijhoff, 1960), vol. 1, pp. 66–69, 111–17.

7) Johannes Linschoten, *Auf dem Weg zu einer Phänomenologischen Psychologie, Die Psychologie von William James* (Berlin: Walter de Gruyter, 1961); English translation, *On The Way Toward a Phenomenological Psychology, The Psychology of William James* (Pittsburgh: Duquesne University Press, 1968).

8) James M. Edie, "Notes on the Philosophical Anthropology of William James," in *An Invitation to Phenomenology* (Chicago: Quadrangle Books, 1965), pp. 110–32.

9) John Wild, "William James and Existential Authenticity," *Journal of Existentialism*, 1965, pp. 243–56.

10) James M. Edie, "William James and the Phenomenology of Religious Experience," in *American Philosophy and the Future*, ed. Michael Novak (New York: Scribner's, 1968), pp. 247–69.

11) Bruce Wilshire, *William James and Phenomenology: A Study of 'The Principles of Psychology'* (Bloomington: Indiana University Press, 1968).

12) John Wild, *The Radical Empiricism of William James* (New York: Doubleday, 1969).

13) Symposium on William James, by James M. Edie, Robert Ehman, and John Wild, in *New Essays in Phenomenology* (Chicago: Quadrangle Books, 1969).

9. William James Earle, "William James," *The Encyclopedia of Philosophy*, ed. Paul Edwards (New York and London: Macmillan, 1967), vol. 4, pp. 240–49. In this essay Earle omits any mention of the recent literature on James written from a phenomenological perspective and furnishes several indications that he wants to forestall, if possible, the effect of this literature: "He [James] was convinced that pure description in the manner of phenomenology is impossible" (p. 242); "Purely phenomenological description being considered impossible by James . . ." (ibid.); "Here again, it must be emphasized that James was not attempting a phenomenology of mental life or consciousness" (p. 243), etc. If these assertions are tested by comparison with the work of Schutz, Gurwitsch, Spiegelberg, Linschoten, Wild, Wilshire, and others considered in this essay, their dogmatic character is striking. Earle gives us no clue as to what he understands by "phenomenology," and his omission of any discussion of James's contribution to the intentional theory of consciousness dates his essay prematurely.

10. *Writings*, pp. xxvii ff.

11. Earle, "William James," p. 244.

12. Husserl's invariable advice to visiting American students at the end of their stay in Freiburg to "study James" has sometimes been misinterpre-

ted in this sense. Husserl himself no doubt felt that the best advice he could give those foreign students who could not be enticed further into phenomenology was to give them an author to read who would put them in some sense on the same path.

13. George Santayana, *Character and Opinion in the United States* (New York: Scribner's, 1920), p. 94.

14. Spiegelberg, *The Phenomenological Movement*, pp. 67, 113.

15. Ibid., p. 112.

16. Ibid., p. 114; see Linschoten, *Auf dem Weg*, p. 18.

17. Cited in Spiegelberg, *The Phenomenological Movement*, p. 114, and in Linschoten, *Auf dem Weg*, p. 17.

18. "Psychologische Studien zur elementaren Logik," *Philosophische Monatshefte* 30, 1894, pp. 159–91. Spiegelberg cites the evidence that Husserl abandoned an early idea of writing a descriptive psychology because he felt "that James had said what he wanted to say" (*The Phenomenological Movement*, pp. 113–14).

19. *Logische Untersuchungen*, 3rd ed. (Halle: Niemeyer, 1922), vol. 2, p. 208.

20. *Die Krisis der Europäischen Wissenschaften un die transzendentale Phänomenologie, Husserliana VI* (The Hague: Nijhoff, 1954), p. 267.

21. Edmund Husserl, "Personliche Aufzeichnungen," *Philosophy and Phenomenological Research*, 1956, pp. 294ff. See also Marvin Farber, *The Foundation of Phenomenology*, 2nd ed. (New York: Paine-Whittman, 1962), p. 277.

22. "If my reading of James is correct, much traditional Jamesian scholarship is faulty: Far too much emphasis has been placed on his later popular philosophy of pragmatism and his occasional pieces in oracular metaphysics, and not enough on his early theory of meaning and on his systematic metaphysics which emerges directly from his conception in the *Principles* of the world of practical realities as a founding level of meaning" (Wilshire, p. 19).

23. Linschoten, p. 16.

24. Wild remarks that "James is not a good summarizer" (p. 200), and this is a defect which James would certainly have acknowledged. He himself referred to the *Principles* as "a loathesome, distented, tumefied, bloated, dropsical mass, testifying to but two facts. *1st*, that there is no such thing as a *science* of psychology, and *2nd*, that W. J. is an incapable" (*Letters*, vol. 1, p. 294). In sending his own "boiled down" version of it (*Psychology, Briefer Course* [New York: Holt, 1892]) to his publisher he wrote: "By adding some twaddle about the senses, by leaving out all polemics and history, all bibliography and experimental details, all metaphysical subtleties and digressions, all quotations, all humour and pathos, all *interest* in short . . . I have produced a tome of pedagogic classic which will enrich both you and me, if not the student's mind" (*Letters*, vol. 1, p. 314). Wild's summaries and critical comments, on the contrary, concern just those "metaphysical subtleties and

digressions" which James left out of the *Briefer Course*, and happily "pass over those sections which are concerned with experimental data" (p. 116). Wild, unlike James, is a good summarizer, and the chapters he devotes to the *Principles* (1–10) extract the phenomenological meat from the text in such a way as to make it almost unnecessary for the student interested in this aspect of James's thought ever to return to the confusions of the *Principles* themselves again. We get from Wild, in consequence, a James considerably more refined and purified than that which faces us in Wilshire's account. Both Wild and Linschoten tend to expound James reverentially, to present him in the best light, and they could be accused of making a concordance of the *Principles*, as Tolstoy did of the Gospels, keeping only those elements an enlightened, contemporary phenomenologist would recognize as sensible, and passing over the rest in silence. Hence Wild's adjectives, describing James's work in the *Principles*, have a laudatory effect while Wilshire's, though based on a similar admiration for James's thought, show repeated exasperation. For Wild, James is almost always "discerning," "painstaking," "penetrating," "extremely perceptive," "remarkable," etc., in the *Principles* (and any harsher adjectives are reserved for the later period [pp. 349, 367ff.]); for Wilshire, it is the James of the *Principles* who is "flawed," "confused," "gross," who makes "glaring," "grievous," and "egregious" mistakes, "blatant contradictions," who "blurs" distinctions, etc. The difference here is not merely one of age and temperament in the respective authors, but in their intentions. Wilshire, as we shall see, is interested in James's "breakthrough" to transcendental phenomenology and focuses his book exclusively on James's approach toward, but hesitant and inconsistent adoption of, a transcendental method. Wild, on the other hand, rejects "transcendental" phenomenology and equates phenomenology with descriptive psychology (cf. pp. 29, 91, 220), and at the same time writes with an eye toward an audience of younger phenomenologists with whom he can persuade to become interested in James's thought (cf. pp. 209ff., 297ff., 352ff., 412ff.). Hence the exhortatory cast of some of Wild's expository sections. Linschoten, on the other hand, takes a more "dialectical" and conciliatory tone than Wilshire (James's contradictions are only "seemingly" contradictory [p. 49], his eclecticism is only "apparent" [p. 54], etc.) but lacks Wild's enthusiasm. He sees James as fitting into a developing school of phenomenological psychologists where he has a well-defined and important place but feels that James's insights have already been taken up by others, clarified, and pushed further along. He situates each of James's theses in the history of psychology, showing what led up to it, and then modifies or corrects each one to the extent necessary to give it an interpretation which is still acceptable and useful for future psychological research. There is no question, for instance, of a "return to James" or anything like that—hence Linschoten's account is the most dispassionate of the three, but it does sometimes leave us with the feeling that this is James as interpreted for the purposes of Johannes Linschoten, the leader of a psychological school, rather than the pure James of history. Nevertheless, each of these studies is of the highest quality and each possesses its own particular validity.

25. Insofar as even this work really *is* systematic. James certainly did not attempt or achieve, even here, a philosophical system. "I . . . have always considered myself," he wrote, "a thing of glimpses, of discontinuity, of *aperçus*, with no power of doing a big job . . ." (*Letters*, vol. 1, p. 295). The numerous paradoxes, inconsistencies, and even contradictions in James's writings have been noted by all his commentators and recognized by himself. What is more important, at the present stage of philosophy, is to know whether at least some of his major theses are not, nevertheless, fully compatible with one another and with a systematic and methodological approach which would incorporate them in a wider viewpoint. It is in that direction that most recent phenomenological work on James is going.

26. In the words of John Dewey this book is as much a classic of philosophy as Locke's *Essay* or Hume's *Treatise* ("The Principles," *Psychological Review*, 1943, p. 121), and even though it is almost unknown at the present time to American psychologists, there are those like Gordon W. Allport who believe the day will come when psychologists will also read it again.

27. Aquinas, to name but one, had produced a whole library of books by the time of his death at the age of forty-nine.

28. This work might conceivably have begun earlier but was delayed by the peculiar accent given to the study of James in America during the early part of this century. E. G. Boring said in 1942 that James's radical empiricism *might* have served as the basis for an American school of phenomenology ("Human Nature vs. Sensations: William James and the Psychology of the Present," *American Journal of Psychology*, 1942, pp. 310–27), and the following year Gordon W. Allport wrote: "Radical empiricism has never become integrated with modern psychology. It might have served as the foundation for an American school of phenomenology, but it did not. Instead, the examination of the intent and constitution of experience was left largely to Husserl and his associates in Germany" ("The Productive Paradoxes of William James," *Psychological Review*, 1943, p. 101).

29. From the first chapter of the *Principles* James adopts "the directedness of mind towards ends" (in the world) as the criterion of mentality, and in chapter nine, on "The Stream of Thought," he lists intentionality in this sense as one of the five essential characters of thought. In 1965 ("Notes on the Philosophical Anthropology of William James," p. 117) I castigated E. G. Boring for omitting this important characteristic from his summary of James's theory of consciousness, but we must note that it was not E. G. Boring but James himself who omitted this characteristic from the "*Four* Characters of Consciousness" listed in the *Briefer Course* (p. 152). Though he never retracts what he says in the *Principles,* he seems to consider this aspect of his discussion to be one of his "metaphysical digressions" which could be conve-

niently removed with the "scissors and paste" job he performed to produce the *Briefer Course*. This is puzzling but further evidence that James did not fully grasp the importance of the distinctions he was making.

30. James refers to Brentano in chapter nine of the *Principles* and some of his expositions here, and later on, are parallel and in some cases almost identical in wording with what Brentano says. Linschoten discusses these parallels but concludes that James's ideas, though parallel, were developed in a way that was essentially new and "his own." Nevertheless, he expresses astonishment that Perry and others not only neglect Husserl but also Brentano and Horwicz whom he explicitly cites in the development of his own theory of consciousness. "This," Linschoten writes, "considering the great similarity and James's quotations, is incomprehensible" (pp. 63ff., 98). It is, no doubt, another indication of the lack of awareness of what was happening in European philosophy on the part of James's American interpreters.

31. Spiegelberg, *The Phenomenological Movement*, p. 115.

32. Ludwig Landgrebe ("Husserls Phanomenologie und die Motive zu ihrer Umbildung," *Revue internationale de philosophie*, 1939) thus develops these distinguishing characteristics from within Husserl's own thought and without reference to James, but his work is supplemented and corrected by that of Spiegelberg, p. 115ff.

33. *Principles*, vol. 1, p. vi. See another concise statement by James of the program which he will ironically and without apologies soon abandon: "*The psychologist's attitude towards cognition* will be so important in the sequel that we must not leave it until it is made perfectly clear. *It is a thoroughgoing dualism.* It supposes two elements, mind knowing and thing known, and treats them as irreducible. Neither gets out of itself or into the other, neither in any way *is* the other, neither *makes* the other. They just stand face to face in a common world, and one simply knows, or is known unto, its counterpart" (*Principles*, vol. 1, p. 218).

34. *Psychology, Briefer Course*, p. 467.

35. Ibid., pp. 464–65. Italics mine.

35. Ibid., p. 468.

37. In the *Principles* James speaks of "metaphysics" in at least three senses. (1) He uses it, especially in the beginning of the work but occasionally throughout, in a most pejorative sense—as something to be avoided at all costs, as something "speculative" (and German), as something which cannot be verified and therefore excessive. (2) Elsewhere, as in chapter twenty-eight, he speaks of metaphysics in the traditional way as the most general science of reality, as a theoretical attempt to bring the whole of experienced reality under *some* general and universal principles. He does not have much faith in such a project, and none at all if metaphysical principles are taken as empirical generalizations, but he is not ready to exclude it altogether. If nature *did* obey such general principles, it *would* be *pro tanto* more intelligible, and it is essential to the mind to keep up this "uneasy" and "striving" ac-

tivity of making the world more intelligible to itself even though we cannot see as yet with any clarity what kind of metaphysical statements would be ultimately acceptable (vol. 2, pp. 669ff.). (3) But in the pages we are referring to, James uses the word "metaphysics" to refer mainly to the theory of knowledge, *Erkenntnistheorie*, to certain distinctions and presuppositions he is forced to examine even though they *should* be excluded by his own empirical program of research. He confessed later, in excising much of this from the *Briefer Course*, that this "metaphysics" was the only "interesting" part of his work but, at the same time, he seems distressed and even angry with himself for having been forced into these analyses. "Metaphysics" in the sense in which he practices it in the *Principles*, then, is not a search for transempirical entities, transempirical causal forces, or universal generalizations, but rather the inescapable investigation of the necessary presuppositions of his psychological program. Such assumptions establish themselves "in our very descriptions of the phenomenal facts" and cannot be left unquestioned. It is not surprising, therefore, that in his examination of these particular assumptions and presuppositions, he accomplishes a kind of phenomenological *epoche* (a search for *Voraussetzungslosigkeit*) which he calls "metaphysics." (Cf. Wilshire, p. 57.) There are writers like William James Earle who misunderstand the sense in which Husserl and other phenomenologists speak of the transcendental attitude as "presuppositionless." They do not mean that any simple, prima facie, description of a matter of fact, such as an act of perception, can be entirely free of presuppositions and assumptions at the outset; it is rather the attempt to uncover the ultimate presuppositions involved in any given experience and thematize them. This is precisely what James is forced to do in his own descriptions.

38. At the beginning of chapter seven of the *Principles* James refers to everything which preceded as "physiological preliminaries" (vol. 1, p. 183).

39. Wilshire, pp. 16–17.

40. Linschoten (pp. 63ff.) cites the few places in which this notion occurs prior to James and Bergson but rightly credits James with being the first to make it a "theory." James is certainly Husserl's source for this and similar locutions.

41. This occurs in chapter nine of the *Principles* on "The Stream of Thought." Wilshire deals with it in chapter four of his book, his best chapter.

42. By the "omnipresence of cognition" James means "reference to an object other than the mental state itself" (*Principles*, vol. 1, p. 186), and this seems to play the same role in his theory of consciousness as what Husserl calls the "presentational" aspect of acts of consciousness in his. According to Husserl, there are other kinds of acts of consciousness than "presentational" (or "cognitive") acts, but all non-presentational acts include and presuppose a presentational act at their basis, whereas the converse is not the case.

43. James deals with the "sense of sameness" which is "the very keel and backbone of our thinking" in explicit detail only in chapter twelve of the *Prin-*

ciples, on "Conception," though much of what he says here is necessary to understand the earlier chapters. This strange inversion of order in James's psychology, according to which he develops only as he goes along the concepts he needs from the beginning, is well brought out in Wilshire's study and shows to what an extent the *Principles* is a work of discovery which led James on and forced him to conclusions of which he had no inkling when he began. (Cf. Wild, pp. 131ff.)

44. Thus Linschoten subtitled his book "On the Way Toward a Phenomenological Psychology," and concluded that the concept of intentionality was "operative" throughout almost the whole of James's writings but that it strangely never became fully "thematic" (p. 186), and Wilshire writes (p. 118): "His dualism collapses—only the rubble remains to clutter the seedbed of phenomenology." This may be overly harsh, but some rubble *does* remain to the end.

45. Wilshire, p. 92.

46. Cf. Schutz, "On Multiple Realities," and Gurwitsch, *The Field of Consciousness*, pp. 379ff.

47. See also the very subtle and complex study of James's conception of the orders of reality with reference to his radical empiricism in Fred Kersten, "Franz Brentano and William James," *Journal of the History of Philosophy*, 1969, pp. 177–91.

48. *The Will to Believe* (New York: Dover, 1956), p. 119.

49. Ibid., p. 43.

50. Jean-Paul Sartre, *Being and Nothingness*, tr. Hazel Barnes (New York: Philosophical Library, 1956), p. xlv.

51. I do not wish in this context to get involved in the delicate issues involved in Wild's criticism of James's later conception of "pure experience" (pp. 361ff.) to which Linschoten, for instance, gives a more sympathetic and phenomenologically acceptable interpretation (pp. 240ff.), but Wild's account has the ring of truth about it—so much the worse for James.

52. Wilshire, pp. 172ff; Wild, pp. 139ff. Wilshire writes (p. 171): "Nowhere in the *Principles* is the force of the phenomenological more evident, and its flowering more nearly complete, than in the chapter 'The Perception of Reality'. Here is his version of the *Lebenswelt*."

53. I have discussed this in greater detail in an article entitled "Ontology Without Metaphysics?" in *The Future of Metaphysics*, ed. Robert E. Wood (Chicago: Quadrangle Books, 1970), pp. 77–97.

54. I have treated this question in somewhat greater detail in Chapter I, "Necessary Truth and Perception: William James on the Structure of Experience." In the *Principles* (vol. 2, p. 320) James indicates that the various orders of experience can be distinguished, correlated and then interrelated only through developing a theory of "contexts." Linschoten (pp. 202ff.) gives a good discussion of the implications of this idea, as does Gurwitsch, *The Field of Consciousness*, part six.

55. Both Wilshire (pp. 200ff.) and Wild (pp. 143ff., 151ff., 159ff., 396ff., 401) place James—I think correctly—closer to "existential" than to "transcendental" phenomenology. They do this because, like Merleau-Ponty, he emphasizes both (1) the "primacy of perception" (and its irreducibility to any idealizing constituting function in its intuitional aspect) and (2) the "embodiment" of consciousness. The difference between them is that whereas Wilshire seems to take this as another indication of James's inability to understand what a truly "transcendental" investigation would be, Wild takes it as an "empiricist" and "realistic" strain in James's thought which is basically more sound than the transcendentalism of Kant and Husserl. For my own part, I think it is necessary to distinguish more clearly the two senses of "transcendental" which we had in Husserl. There is the basically "Kantian" sense, which Husserl adopts (with modifications which do not concern us here) in his eidetic analysis: the elaboration of the necessary conditions which account for the possibility of a given phenomenon. This is the element of "conceptual analysis" which is involved in turning from a given factual instance of conscious experience to its *essential structure*. This sense of "transcendental" is accepted by Merleau-Ponty, Ricoeur, and other "existential" phenomenologists no less than by Husserl; without it no phenomenology of perception, of will, of imagination, or any other realm of experience would be possible at all. The second sense of "transcendental" occurs in Husserl when he speaks of the "transcendental-phenomenological" reduction as a re-tracing of noematic structures of "objects" of experience to their sources in the "constituting" acts of "pure" consciousness. It is this second project of "transcendental" analysis which Merleau-Ponty, for one, argues cannot be "completed" (*Phenomenology of Perception*, tr. Colin Smith [New York: Humanities Press, 1962], p. xiv). It cannot be completed because the very notion of the "phenomenon" eidetically implies a transcendent "something" which is intuitively experienced as well as transphenomenal "subject" which does the experiencing, and, further, this "subject"—at least in perceptual experience—is a "body-subject" rather than a pure, disembodied ego. Therefore, even those of us who are disposed to agree with Wild that the second kind of reduction is incompatible with a "radically empiricist" method in philosophy, will still agree with Wilshire that "in becoming existential, phenomenology need not become non-transcendental" (in the first, or "eidetic" sense). (Cf. Wilshire, p. 203.) There is, of course, neither an eidetic nor a transcendental-phenomenological reduction in James in any *strict* sense.

56. "James's Chapter Ten on the self is dramatic. We see a thinker on the move, too honest to dissemble, who startles himself with his own discoveries. In this respect it is comparable to the internal books of Aristotle's *Metaphysics*. Here James catches himself in the act, as it were, of procrastinating, of postponing urgent issues" (Wilshire, p. 124).

57. Wilshire, p. 125. I follow Wilshire closely in setting up this problem, but much less closely in the analysis of its solution. Cf. Jean-Paul Sartre, *Sit-*

uations I (Paris: Gallimard, 1947), pp. 31–35: "Against the digestive philosophy of empirio-criticism, of neo-Kantianism, against all 'psychologism' . . . Husserl sees in consciousness an irreducible fact which cannot be rendered by any physical image, except, perhaps, the rapid and obscure image of bursting forth. To know, is 'to burst out towards', to tear oneself away from the clammy gastric depths to slip outside of oneself over there, towards what is not oneself. . . . Now, consciousness is purified, it is as clear as a strong wind, there is nothing left in it, except a movement of escaping itself, a slipping outside of itself. If, by an impossible chance, you were to get "inside" a consciousness, you would be seized by a whirlwind and thrown back outside . . . for consciousness has no 'inside'."

58. Jean-Paul Sartre, *The Transcendence of the Ego*, tr. Forrest Williams and Robert Kirkpatrick (New York: Noonday Press, 1957). Aron Gurwitsch, "A Non-Egological Conception of Consciousness," in *Studies in Phenomenology and Psychology*, pp. 287–300. Though on this and a few other points we will mention Sartre and James hold similar positions, Sartre nowhere takes cognizance of James's writings. Unlike the founder of phenomenology, the epigoni of Husserl, and especially the French, live their philosophical lives for the most part in an isolation from American thought as complete and one-sided as we have found to be the case in the American commentators on James. James, to be sure, is a name known to all French philosophers because of his relations with Bergson and because he is on the syllabus of readings for the baccalaureate in philosophy in French lycées. But, as the writings of Sartre and Merleau-Ponty attest, the only thing the ordinary French philosopher seems to retain from this exposure is the unfortunate James-Lange theory of the emotions. (Cf. also Wilshire, p. 212.)

59. Cf. *The Transcendence of the Ego*, pp. 96–97; "The *me* being an object, it is evident that I shall never be able to say: *my* consciousness, that is the consciousness of my *me* (save in a purely designative sense, as one says for example: the day of *my* baptism). The ego is not the owner of consciousness; it is the object of consciousness. To be sure, we constitute spontaneously our states and actions as productions of the ego. But our states and actions are also objects. We never have a direct intuition of the spontaneity of an instantaneous consciousness as produced by the ego. . . ."

60. James, like Sartre, provides in his analysis of the plurality of "selves" with which consciousness endows itself the basis for a phenomenological theory of acting, role-playing, and enactment which has been only partially exploited up to present time. It is not developed in any of the literature cited in this article.

61. In the *Principles* (vol. 1, p. 305) James cites an article by M. Souriau (*Revue Philosophique*, 1886, pp. 449–72) entitled "La Conscience de Soi" in which Souriau argues for the conclusion "que la conscience n'existe pas." James tells us in the *Essays in Radical Empiricism* of how this idea grew on him over the years until he also came to the conclusion that consciousness is

"nothing," the "name of a non-entity," which must be replaced by its "equivalent in realities of experience" (*Writings*, p. 169).

62. Jean-Paul Sartre, *Les Temps Modernes* 1, 1945, p. 7.

63. Linschoten, pp. 212ff.; Wilshire, pp. 133ff.; Wild, pp. 80ff.

64. "The Experience of Activity," in *Writings*, p. 284.

65. See the parallel passage in *Essays in Radical Empiricism:* "I believe that 'consciousness', when once it has evaporated to this estate of pure diaphaneity, is on the point of disappearing altogether. It is the name of a nonentity, and has no right to a place among first principles. Those who still cling to it are clinging to a mere echo, the faint rumor left behind by the disappearing 'soul' upon the air of philosophy. . . . It seems to me that the hour is ripe for it to be openly and universally discarded (*Writings*, p. 169).

66. Cf. *The Transcendence of the Ego*, pp. 37–40. "It is ordinarily thought that the existence of a transcendental *I* may be justified by the need that consciousness has for unity and individuality. It is because all my perceptions and all my thoughts refer themselves back to this permanent seat that my consciousness is unified. It is because I can say *my* consciousness, and because Peter and Paul can also speak of *their* consciousness, that these consciousnesses distinguish themselves from each other. The *I* is the product of inwardness. . . . But it is precisely Husserl who has no need of such a principle. The object is transcendent to the consciousnesses which grasp it, and it is in the object that the unity of the consciousnesses is found. . . . It is consciousness which unifies itself, concretely, by a play of 'transversal' intentionalities which are concrete and real retentions of past consciousnesses. Thus consciousness refers perpetually to itself. . . . Consequently we may reply without hesitation: the phenomenological conception of consciousness renders the unifying and individualizing role of the *I* totally useless. It is consciousness, on the contrary which makes possible the unity and the personality of my *I*." It would seem that Husserl's remark that, for James, consciousness is essentially "anonymous" is quite exact. (Cf. *Krisis*, p. 267.)

67. James once said that the true line of philosophical progress lies not so much through Kant as around him (see note 6 above). Wilshire argues convincingly (pp. 190ff.) that James did not grasp clearly the "transcendental" character of Kant's argument. When Kant says that "The *I think* must be capable of accompanying all our representations," he is making a conceptual as opposed to a factual point, namely, that it is of the essence of experience, or thought, that an "object" of thought be presented to some experiencer (i.e., what the concept of experience means is that there *be* an experiencer and correlatively something experienced, and for an experiencer to *be* an experiencer he must be capable not only of knowing *what* but of knowing *that* he is experiencing). I agree with Wilshire that James did not sufficiently appreciate the point that Kant was making (cf. *Principles*, vol. 1, pp. 361ff.), but it may also be that, like Sartre, he does not intend to deny in any way this ("empty") Kantian principle but rather to discover the root of its apriority in

experience itself. Sartre writes in a similar vein: "The critical problem being one of validity, Kant says nothing concerning the actual existence of the *I think*. On the contrary, he seems to have seen perfectly well that there are moments of consciousness without the *I*, for he says '*must be able* to accompany'. . . . For Kant, transcendental consciousness is nothing but the set of conditions which are necessary for the existence of an empirical consciousness. . . . But [the phenomenological question] is actually a question of fact, which may be formulated thus: is the *I* that we encounter in our consciousness made possible by the synthetic unity of our representations, or is it the *I* which in fact unites the representations to each other?" (*The Transcendence of the Ego*, pp. 32–34.)

68. Cf. *The Transcendence of the Ego*, pp. 44–45. "But it must be remembered that all the writers who have described the *Cogito* have dealt with it as a reflective operation. . . . Such a *Cogito* is performed by a consciousness *directed upon consciousness*, a consciousness which takes consciousness as an object. . . . But the fact remains that we are in the presence of two consciousnesses, one of which is consciousness *of* the other. Thus the essential principle of phenomenology, 'all consciousness is consciousness *of* something', is preserved. Now, my reflecting consciousness does not take itself for an object when I effect the *Cogito*. What it affirms concerns the reflected consciousness. Insofar as my reflecting consciousness is consciousness of itself, it is *non-positional* consciousness. It becomes positional only by directing itself upon the reflected consciousness which itself was not a positional consciousness of itself before being reflected. Thus the consciousness which says *I Think* is precisely not the consciousness which thinks."

69. Sartre, *Being and Nothingness*, pp. lxi 67.

70. *The Will to Believe*, p. 204, in the essay entitled "The Moral Philosopher and the Moral Life."

71. Cf. Wilshire, p. 178. Wilshire here follows and interprets Wild, with whom he is in agreement.

72. It would be no exaggeration to say that James became a philosopher over the problem of free will and determinism; the great personal crisis of his life was solved through the realization that though he could find no intellectual refutation of determinism, he experienced his freedom to act, on himself, on others, on the world. Cf. "Notes on the Philosophical Anthropology of William James," pp. 131ff. It might be relevant to note a similar "decisional" element in Sartre's view of freedom: "Those who hide from this total freedom, in a guise of solemnity or with deterministic excuses, I shall call cowards. . . ." in "Existentialism is a Humanism," *Existentialism from Dostoevsky to Sartre*, ed. Walter Kaufmann (New York: The New American Library, Meridian, 1957), p. 308.

73. *Letters*, vol. 1, p. 147.

74. Cf. Edmund Husserl, *Cartesian Meditations*, tr. Dorion Cairns (The Hague: Nijhoff, 1960), pp. 60ff., 77, 135, and Maurice Merleau-Ponty,

Signs, tr. Richard C. McCleary (Evanston: Northwestern University Press, 1964), p. 88 and *passim.*

75. Cf. especially *Humanisme et terreur* (Paris: Gallimard, 1947), chapter 2.

76. My only major disagreement with Wild's discussion of James's contribution to the phenomenology of religious experience lies in his connecting this approach with that "of later phenomenologists of religion" like G. Van der Leeuw (p. 316). I find that the so-called "phenomenologists of religion" (Van der Leeuw, Wach, Otto, Eliade) have taken a title to themselves which very inexactly describes their program; since they are concerned with the history of symbols and institutions rather than primary experience, it seems to me a misnomer to call this phenomenology. James, on the contrary, did adopt an authentically phenomenological approach (without the title) and has had almost no successors in this endeavor up to the present moment. See my article, "William James and the Phenomenology of Religious Experience," pp. 249ff.

77. Margaret Knight, *William James* (London: Penguin Books, 1950), p. 50.

78. *Letters,* vol. 1, p. 153, cited by Linschoten, p. 312.

III. William James's Phenomenology of Religious Experience

1. I am undertaking this study in the same spirit as one published earlier under the title "Notes on the Philosophical Anthropology of William James," *Invitation to Phenomenology* (Chicago: Quadrangle Books, 1965), pp. 110–32.

2. In some of his later writings, however, Husserl did speculate on whether his teleological conception of (transpersonal) consciousness might not imply an *absolute ideale Polidee* which might be called "God," more in a Whiteheadian sense of a Becoming God than in the Kantian sense. Stephen Strasser has collected most of the material left us by Husserl on this subject and published it in an excellent article, "Das Gottesproblem in der Spätphilosophie Edmund Husserls," in *Philosophisches Jahrbuch,* vol. 67. On Husserl's own attitude toward religion, cf. also Herbert Spiegelberg, *The Phenomenological Movement* (The Hague: Nijhoff, 1960), vol. 1, pp. 85–87.

3. Cf. Martin Heidegger, *Letter on Humanism,* tr. Edgar Lohner, in *Philosophy in the Twentieth Century,* ed. Henry D. Aiken and William Barrett (New York: Random House, 1962), vol. 11, pp. 294ff.

4. Cf. Pierre Thévénaz, *What Is Phenomenology?* (Chicago: Quadrangle Books, 1962), pp. 80ff.

5. Cf. Maurice Merleau-Ponty, *The Primacy of Perception* (Evanston: Northwestern University Press, 1964), pp. 35ff., and *In Praise of Philosophy* (Evanston: Northwestern University Press, 1963), pp. 41ff.

6. Cf. Herbert Spiegelberg, *The Phenomenological Movement,* vol. 1,

pp. 10–11, vol. 2, pp. 605–606. As will become clear in the sequel, I agree with Spiegelberg's view that it would be misleading "to confuse a mere typology of religious institutions with a phenomenology in the philosophical sense, which concentrates on the religious acts and contents in religious experience and explores their essential structures and relationships."

7. G. Van Der Leeuw, *Religion in Essence and Manifestation (Phänomenologie der Religion)* (New York: Harper Torchbooks, 1963), p. 674 n.

8. The studies by Joachim Wach are distinguished from those of Mircea Eliade chiefly by the fact that Wach was primarily interested in establishing a "typology" of the sociological institutions of religion whereas Eliade is primarily concerned with elucidating the universal religious symbols, anterior to reflection, through which the world is constituted as "real" and "sacred" to man. Cf. Mircea Eliade, "Methodological Remarks on the Study of Religious Symbolism," in *The History of Religions*, ed. Mircea Eliade and Joseph M. Kitagawa (Chicago: University of Chicago Press, 1959), pp. 86–107; and *Images and Symbols* (London: Harvill Press, 1961). Wach makes his most explicit statements on methodology in *The Comparative Study of Religions* (New York: Columbia University Press, 1958), though there are some methodological sections in *Types of Religious Experience* (Chicago: University of Chicago Press, 1951), and in earlier works. Van Der Leeuw's discussion of methodology is given in the somewhat unsatisfactory and confusing form of an appendix, "Epilegomena," to the second edition of his *Phänomenologie der Religion*.

9. Van Der Leeuw, *Religion*, p. 673.

10. Wach, *The Comparative Study of Religions*, pp. 24–25.

11. Van Der Leeuw takes care to distinguish the "phenomenology of religion" from what it is not: namely, a poetics of religion, the history of religion, the psychology of religion, the philosophy of religion, or, finally, theology (*Religion*, pp. 685–88). His more positive statement as to just what it is, is much less satisfactory.

12. Ibid., p. 677; Wach, *Religionswissenschaft* (Leipzig: J. C. Hinrichs, 1924), p. 117; Eliade, "Methodological Remarks," pp. 88ff.

13. Henry Duméry criticizes this group of authors in a similar manner: "M. Joachim Wach . . . tout en se réclamant de la typologie, a le souci d'une methode normative. Sa facon de classer les grandes formes de l'expérience religieuse aboutit en fait à un choix fort raisonnable. Mais elle ne s'appuie guere sur des criteres philosophiquement élabores. On peut en dire autant de Van Der Leeuw et d'Eliade, dont les travaux sont par ailleurs extremement précieux" (*Critique et Religion* [Paris: Sedes, 1957], p. 204).

14. While the great contrast between James's approach to religious experience and that of the school of the "phenomenology of religion" is evident, and while James presents a much more authentically phenomenological approach (taken in the general sense of Husserl and Merleau-Ponty), I do not want to make the absurd claim that James thus becomes *illico presto* a pure

Husserlian. He had almost no knowledge of Husserl and, in many ways, was almost an exact opposite in philosophical temperament. In a letter to Stumpf he once wrote: "I . . . have an *apriori* distrust of all attempts at making philosophy systematically exact just now. The frequency with which a man loves to use the words *streng wissenschaftlich* is beginning to be for me a measure of the shallowness of his sense of truth. Altogether, the less we have to say about *Strenge* the better . . ." (Ralph Barton Perry, *The Thought and Character of William James* [Boston: Little, Brown, 1935], vol. 2, p. 185). Thus it would be wrong to attempt to force James's own work into the mold of a strictly "scientific" phenomenological investigation as Husserl conceived it. James's phenomenology, if it can be called that (and I am arguing that it can), is of a much more general sort, and would certainly fall within what Alfred Schutz has called "the phenomenology of the natural attitude"—but then so does a very large part of the phenomenology which has been undertaken by the disciples of Husserl themselves. In what follows I limit myself strictly to James, while pointing out what appear to me to be certain undeniable affinities, parallels, similarities, and convergencies with the phenomenological method strictly so called. It remains that James could perhaps have prosecuted the kind of study he had in mind, free both of psychologism and metaphysics, with greater economy and precision if he had been aware of some of the conditions of eidetic analysis as established by Husserl.

15. Perry, *Thought and Character*, vol. 1, p. 165.

16. Of James's personal attitude toward religion Perry writes: "James's religion took the form neither of dogma nor of institutional allegiance. He was essentially a man of faith, though not a man for any one church or creed against the rest. Unlike his father, he was not interested in the elaboration and specific formulation even of his own personal beliefs" (vol. 2, p. 358).

17. Ibid., p. 239, from the original opening paragraph of the Gifford Lectures.

18. This study is, then, no attempt whatever to systematize James's religious philosophy; it is, moreover, quite strictly limited to the method established in *The Varieties of Religious Experience*, though I have had in mind as well the few places in his other works where he touches on this problem.

19. *The Varieties of Religious Experience, a Study in Human Nature* (New York: Mentor Books, 1958), p. 33. Page numbers given in the text hereafter refer to this edition of James's work.

20. James does not, of course, actually mention either Luther or Solovyov in this connection, but I am confident that this would be his attitude, as it is mine, to their post-Freudian debunkers. Cf. *Varieties*, p. 316: "To the medical mind these ecstasies signify nothing but suggested and imitated hypnoid states, on an intellectual basis of superstition, and a corporeal one of degeneration and hysteria. Undoubtedly these pathological conditions have existed in many and possibly in all cases, but that fact tells us nothing

about the value for knowledge of the consciousness which they induce. To pass a spiritual judgment upon these states, we must not content ourselves with superficial medical talk, but inquire into their fruits for life."

21. James nevertheless remained a child of his Victorian period in several respects. He shows no knowledge of, or sensitivity whatever to, the major nineteenth-century critique of Christianity begun by such thinkers as Feuerbach, Nietzsche, Dostoevski, and Kierkegaard. One of his few references to Nietzsche links him with Schopenhauer and then James says that at least half their writings seem to him "the sick shriekings of two dying rats" (p. 47). In his writings on religion as elsewhere, for all his use of pathological and neurotic material, James remains an optimist and fails to see the "dark side" of the religious question, the problem of the radical alienation of man in contemporary civilization. In this one respect James is much less of a prophet than Nietzsche, whom he clearly did not understand. He even seems to think that Nietzsche's attack on the Christian notion of sainthood was due to his being a "carnal man" (p. 286).

22. Bertrand Russell, *Why I Am Not a Christian* (New York: Simon & Schuster, 1957), p. 24.

23. Gordon W. Allport in *The Individual and His Religion* (New York: Macmillan, 1950), develops some of these suggestions by James in an extremely interesting and creative way, without, however, undertaking the task of a full-fledged continuation of the project of a phenomenology of religious experience. See especially his discussion "Is There a Single Form of Religious Sentiment?" pp. 3ff.

24. Maurice Merleau-Ponty, "La conscience et l'acquisition du langage," *Bulletin de psychologie*, November 1964, p. 229.

25. Perry, vol. 2, p. 354.

IV. Notes on the Philosophical Anthropology of William James

1. In writing these lines I have had in mind such accounts of James's philosophy as those found in the following: Emile Boutroux, *William James* (Paris: Colin, 1912); Emile Boutroux, *La pensée américaine et la pensée française* (Paris: Colin, 1913); Jean Wahl, *Les philosophies pluralistes d'Angleterre et d'Amérique* (Paris: Alcan, 1920); Emmanuel Leroux, *Le pragmatisme américain et anglais* (Paris: Alcan, 1922); Horace Kallen, *The Philosophy of William James* (New York: Random House, Modern Library, 1925); Sidney Hook, *The Metaphysics of Pragmatism* (Chicago: Open Court, 1927); Ralph Barton Perry, *In the Spirit of William James* (New Haven: Yale University Press, 1938); Émile Brehier, *Histoire de la philosophie* (Paris: Presses Universitaires de France, 1948); Gerard Deledalle, *Histoire de la philosophie américaine* (Paris: Presses Universitaires de France, 1954); Morton White, *The Age of Analysis* (New York: The New American Library, Mentor Books,

1955); Edward C. Moore, *American Pragmatism* (New York: Columbia University Press, 1961), and others. This list, which could be extended indefinitely, is given as a fair sample only.

2. *Some Problems of Philosophy*, published posthumously in 1911 in fragmentary form.

3. Brehier, *Histoire*, p. 1045.

4. The reasons that have been given for this are various and range from James's unwillingness to be "tyrannized over" by a book the way he had been under "the shadow of that interminable black cloud," *The Principles*, to the fact that he simply liked people and lecturing to popular audiences more than writing systematic philosophy (Moore, *American Pragmatism*, p. 110). I think the better explanation is that James was not a systematic philosopher but, as he says himself, "a thing of glimpses, of discontinuity, of *aperçus*, with no power of doing a big job" (*Letters*, vol. 1, p. 295). In short, James was an "empiricist" or "phenomenologist" who eschewed grand systems for minute, groping, partial investigations of limited scope. This does not mitigate our loss of any attempt to unify and systematize these disparate studies *after the fact* so to speak. This task, which James himself avoided, has been only very indifferently taken up by his successors, and now it is impossible even to consider such an undertaking without carrying each of James's particular studies far beyond the point where he himself left it.

5. Cf. principally: Aron Gurwitsch, *La théorie du champ de la conscience* (Paris: Desdée de Brouwer, 1957); Alfred Schutz, *Collected Papers* (The Hague: Nijhoff, 1962) vol. 1; Herbert Spiegelberg, *The Phenomenological Movement* (The Hague: Nijhoff, 1960), vol. 1, pp. 111–17 and *passim*; John Wild, *Existence and the World of Freedom* (Englewood Cliffs, N.J.: Prentice-Hall, 1963) passim; Johannes Linschoten, *Auf dem Weg zu einer phänomenologischen Psychologie, Die Psychologie von William James* (Berlin: Walter de Gruyter, 1961).

6. Linschoten, *Auf dem Weg*. The value of this book is great and it is impossible to question either its philosophical or historical validity. It will seem a strange-sounding book to those who have remained unaware of James's influence on European phenomenology, but this only points up the need for such a book and we express the hope that it will be speedily translated into English. However, in his effort to situate James within the phenomenological tradition, to understand his philosophy in a phenomenological sense, and to give him the proper credit for the influence of his insights, the author of this work goes so far toward making James speak the language of Husserl that certain radical differences are blurred. On the whole, however, it cannot be denied that this is the best *recent* work on the philosophy of William James, and perhaps the best which has been written up to now.

7. *Essays in Radical Empiricism* (New York: Longmans, Green & Co., 1942), p. 42.

8. *The Principles of Psychology* (New York: Henry Holt, 1890), vol. 1, pp. 245–46.

9. Moore, p. 71.

10. Note, however, that James *did* conceive of consciousness as "intentional" in a sense similar to Husserl's, though he did not emphasize this aspect of it or make it *the* central element of his theory of mind. Cf. *Principles*, vol. 1, pp. 271ff. This aspect of James's thought so little impressed itself on his followers that when Edwin G. Boring summarizes James's theory of consciousness ("The Stream of Thought") in his *History of Experimental Psychology* (New York: Appleton-Century Crofts, 1957), pp. 513ff., he lists only four of the five characteristics of consciousness which James had given, and the one he omits is "intentionality" or "world-directedness."

11. Ralph Barton Perry, *The Thought and Character of William James* (Boston: Little, Brown, 1935), vol. 2, p. 435: "My starting point is, of course, the doctrine of immediate perception. . . ."

12. *Principles*, vol. 1, pp. 276.

13. Ibid., p. 271, and *The Meaning of Truth* (New York: Longmans, Green, & Co., 1909), p. 217 and passim.

14. This statement rests on the interpretation of James's view of "radical empiricism" which I believe to be the most sound; I do not therefore accept Perry's "metaphysical" interpretation of James's last period (*In the Spirit of William James*, pp. 77ff.). There *is* a metaphysics within James's radical empiricism, but it is not at all Machian. It is only fair to point out that Perry does not attribute Mach's thesis explicitly to James but this seems to be his understanding of his metaphysics.

15. However, we cannot be sure to what extent the dominant "idealistic" interpretation of Husserl is justified, since those who have studied his unpublished manuscripts and especially those of his final period have a very different view of Husserl's philosophy than those who have concentrated on his "middle period" publications. We cannot enter into this question here, but it is possible that the final Husserl is not as far from James as is, for instance, the Husserl of *Ideen I*, or the Husserl of the *Cartesian Meditations*.

16. Perry, *In the Spirit of William James*, pp. 119ff.

17. Aron Gurwitsch criticizes James's notion of "pure experience" (*Théorie du champ de la conscience*, pp. 31ff.) as a completely unstructured, blooming, buzzing, chaotic mass without even any implicit organization prior to the intervention of the "selective interest" of the experiencer. But James holds this view of "pure experience" only for "newborn babies," for "men in semi-coma from sleep, drugs, illnesses or blows" (*Essays in Radical Empiricism*, p. 93). For all other persons experience is unstructured rather in the sense that it is "ambiguous" and always changing, but it is not a chaotic spray of impressions in a Humean or Kantian sense. If the subject itself is strictly correlative to the object of his experiences, and if the organization of experi-

ence involves this primary interaction, then James's theory does not seem to be as far from either that of Merleau-Ponty or that of Gurwitsch himself as the latter declares it to be.

18. *Essays in Radical Empiricism*, p. 160.

19. Gurwitsch, *La théorie*, p. 29.

20. *The Will to Believe* (New York: Longmans, Green & Co., 1897), p. 54.

21. *Principles*, vol. 2, p. 295.

22. Ibid., p. 297.

23. Henry Veatch, "Matrix, Matter and Method in Metaphysics," *Review of Metaphysics*, 1961, p. 589: "Now I ask you, even for a Frenchman, and even for a Frenchman who professes and looks down upon the world from such an academic pinnacle as the Collège de France, would it not be going just a little bit far for such a man to act and behave and live as if he were *the absolute source?*"

24. "Humanism and Truth" in the Meridian edition of *Pragmatism* (New York: 1955), p. 250.

25. Though James let himself be argued out of his famous title, *The Will to Believe*, and in a moment of weakness admitted to his critics that he ought to have entitled the work "The Right to Believe," he nevertheless kept the original title up to the end and came back to it in his last work. This aspect of his thought vindicates more than the "right" to believe.

26. "The Sentiment of Rationality" in *The Will to Believe*, p. 64.

27. *Principles*, vol. 2, pp. 283–89.

28. "The Sentiment of Rationality," p. 72, quoting Schopenhauer.

29. "Humanism and Truth," p. 244.

30. Ibid., p. 246.

31. I have particularly in mind an unpublished paper on the phenomenology of the self read by Professor Herbert Spiegelberg at the meeting of the American Philosophical Association, Western Division, on May 2, 1963, at Columbus, Ohio.

32. *Principles*, vol. 1, p. 301.

33. Ibid., p. 322.

34. Ibid., p. 333.

35. Ibid., pp. 289–90.

36. Ibid., pp. 226ff.

37. Ibid., p. 341, "nothing can be known *about* it till it be dead and gone."

38. *Essays in Radical Empiricism*, pp. 3–4.

39. Though the argument I give here is biographical, much more evidence for this view could be adduced. I do not believe the method of what Professor William Earle calls "ontological autobiography" (cf. "Phenomenology and Existentialism" in *Journal of Philosophy*, 1960, pp. 75ff.) is the most important or the most telling, and I certainly do not consider it the exclusive

philosophical method, but at the same time I do believe that it has great value and is not to be dismissed simply as the "sociology of philosophy." In the present instance it is used mainly as a shortcut.

40. Horace Kallen is correct in saying that "What healed William James was then not medicine. . . . What healed him was the attainment of his philosophy" (*The Philosophy of William James*, p. 30). But we must remember that, at this point, James had no philosophy as yet in the sense of explicit philosophical positions or doctrines. His philosophy lay in the future; what he had discovered was his fundamental fact, his starting point, the *free act*.

41. *Letters,* vol. 1, pp. 47, 169–70.

Selected Bibliography

By William James

Essays in Radical Empiricism and a Pluralistic Universe. New York: Longmans, Green & Co., 1942.

Essays on Faith and Morals. Edited by Ralph Barton Perry. Cleveland: Meridian Books, 1962.

Human Immortality: Two Supposed Objections to the Doctrine. Boston: Houghton, Mifflin & Co., 1898.

Letters of William James. Edited by Henry James, 2 vols. Boston: The Atlantic Monthly Press, 1920.

The Letters of William James and Theodore Flournoy. Edited by Robert C. LeClair. Madison: University of Wisconsin Press, 1966.

The Meaning of Truth: A Sequel to Pragmatism. New York: Longmans, Green & Co., 1909, 1911.

Memories and Studies. New York: Longmans, Green & Co., 1911, 1924.

Pragmatism. New York: World Publishing Company, 1955.

The Principles of Psychology. 2 vols. New York: Henry Holt and Company, 1890. Dover, 1950.

Some Problems of Philosophy. New York: Longmans, Green & Co., 1948.

Talks to Teachers on Psychology, and to Students on Some of Life's Ideals. New York: Henry Holt and Co., 1899.

The Varieties of Religious Experience. New York: Longmans, Green & Co., 1902. Modern Library, no date.

William James: The Essential Writings. Edited by Bruce W. Wilshire with a Preface by James M. Edie. New York: Harper Torchbooks, 1971.

The Will to Believe. New York: Longmans, Green & Co., 1897. Dover, 1956.

The Writings of William James. Edited with an Introduction by John J. McDermott. New York: Random House, 1967.

About William James

Applan, Gay W. *William James, A Biography.* New York: Viking, 1967.

Gurwitsch, Aron. *The Field of Consciousness.* Pittsburgh: Duquesne University Press, 1964.

106

Kallen, Horace M. *The Philosophy of William James*. New York: Modern Library, 1925.

Linschoten, Hans. *On the Way Toward a Phenomenological Psychology, The Psychology of William James*. Pittsburgh: Duquesne University Press, 1968.

Perry, Ralph Barton. *The Thought and Character of William James*. 2 vols. Boston: Little, Brown, 1935–36.

Schutz, Alfred. *Collected Papers*, Vol. I. Edited by Maurice Natanson, with a Preface by Herman-Leo Van Breda. The Hague: Nijhoff, 1962.

Wild, John. *The Radical Empiricism of William James*. New York: Doubleday, 1969.

Wilshire, Bruce. *William James and Phenomenology: A Study of "The Principles of Psychology."* Bloomington: Indiana University Press, 1968.

Index